# EP Literature and Composition II Vocabulary Workbook

This book belongs to:

_____

# EP Literature and Composition II Vocabulary Workbook

This book, made by Tina Rutherford with permission from Easy Peasy All-in-One Homeschool, is based on the Literature and Composition II component of Easy Peasy's curriculum. For EP's online curriculum visit allinonehighschool.com

All definitions taken from WordNet – commercial use granted.
Princeton University "About WordNet." wordnet.princeton.edu. Princeton University. 2010.
WordNet 3.0 Copyright 2006 by Princeton University. All rights reserved.

Cover design by Yuletide Media: www.yuletidemedia.com

Lovingly edited by Holly Dunn

ISBN: 9798443996097

First Edition: April, 2022

# About this Book

This is an offline version of the vocabulary portion of Easy Peasy All-in-One High School's Literature and Composition II course. We've modified and expanded upon the online activities and printable worksheets available at the Easy Peasy All-in-One High School website (allinonehighschool.com) so that you can work offline if desired. This book is ONLY the vocabulary component of Literature and Composition II. It will not include any of the reading, writing, or other language arts assignments and is not a complete English course on its own.

# How to use this Book

This book is designed to be used in conjunction with the Literature and Composition II Readers and Language Arts workbook (for a full offline course) OR alongside the online Literature and Composition II course. As you proceed through this book, you will use the other Literature and Composition II books or the online assignments to fill out the rest of the assignments for a full high school English credit.

This book follows the EP online Literature and Composition II course in sequential order, providing an offline version of the vocabulary assignments. A student completing the assignments in this book along with the other Literature and Composition II books or the other online assignments will complete one full high school English course.

Each five-lesson week will have a vocabulary unit. The first three lessons of the week will present the vocabulary words. Read them out loud and use them in sentences. The fourth lesson will be an activity to help drill in the vocabulary words. The fifth lesson will be a graded quiz. There will be review from time to time.

# Completion Chart for Lessons 1 - 45

| | | | | | |
|---|---|---|---|---|---|
| (1) | Unit 1 | (16) | Units 1-3 review | (31) | Unit 6 |
| (2) | Unit 1 | (17) | Units 1-3 review | (32) | Unit 6 |
| (3) | Unit 1 | (18) | Units 1-3 review | (33) | Unit 6 |
| (4) | Unit 1 practice | (19) | Units 1-3 review | (34) | Unit 6 practice |
| (5) | Unit 1 quiz | (20) | Units 1-3 quiz | (35) | Unit 6 quiz |
| (6) | Unit 2 | (21) | Unit 4 | (36) | Units 4-6 review |
| (7) | Unit 2 | (22) | Unit 4 | (37) | Units 4-6 review |
| (8) | Unit 2 | (23) | Unit 4 | (38) | Units 4-6 review |
| (9) | Unit 2 practice | (24) | Unit 4 practice | (39) | Units 4-6 review |
| (10) | Unit 2 quiz | (25) | Unit 4 quiz | (40) | Units 4-6 quiz |
| (11) | Unit 3 | (26) | Unit 5 | (41) | Unit 7 |
| (12) | Unit 3 | (27) | Unit 5 | (42) | Unit 7 |
| (13) | Unit 3 | (28) | Unit 5 | (43) | Unit 7 |
| (14) | Unit 3 practice | (29) | Unit 5 practice | (44) | Unit 7 practice |
| (15) | Unit 3 quiz | (30) | Unit 5 quiz | (45) | Unit 7 quiz |

# Completion Chart for Lessons 46 - 90

| | | | | | |
|---|---|---|---|---|---|
| (46) | Unit 8 | (61) | Unit 10 | (76) | Units 10-12 review |
| (47) | Unit 8 | (62) | Unit 10 | (77) | Units 10-12 review |
| (48) | Unit 8 | (63) | Unit 10 | (78) | Units 10-12 review |
| (49) | Unit 8 practice | (64) | Unit 10 practice | (79) | Units 10-12 review |
| (50) | Unit 8 quiz | (65) | Unit 10 quiz | (80) | Units 10-12 quiz |
| (51) | Unit 9 | (66) | Unit 11 | (81) | Unit 13 |
| (52) | Unit 9 | (67) | Unit 11 | (82) | Unit 13 |
| (53) | Unit 9 | (68) | Unit 11 | (83) | Unit 13 |
| (54) | Unit 9 practice | (69) | Unit 11 practice | (84) | Unit 13 practice |
| (55) | Unit 9 quiz | (70) | Unit 11 quiz | (85) | Unit 13 quiz |
| (56) | Units 7-9 review | (71) | Unit 12 | (86) | Unit 14 |
| (57) | Units 7-9 review | (72) | Unit 12 | (87) | Unit 14 |
| (58) | Units 7-9 review | (73) | Unit 12 | (88) | Unit 14 |
| (59) | Units 7-9 review | (74) | Unit 12 practice | (89) | Unit 14 practice |
| (60) | Units 7-9 quiz | (75) | Unit 12 quiz | (90) | Unit 14 quiz |

# Completion Chart for Lessons 91-135

| | | | | | |
|---|---|---|---|---|---|
| (91) | Unit 15 | (106) | Unit 16 | (121) | Units 16-18 review |
| (92) | Unit 15 | (107) | Unit 16 | (122) | Units 16-18 review |
| (93) | Unit 15 | (108) | Unit 16 | (123) | Units 16-18 review |
| (94) | Unit 15 practice | (109) | Unit 16 practice | (124) | Units 16-18 review |
| (95) | Unit 15 quiz | (110) | Unit 16 quiz | (125) | Units 16-18 quiz |
| (96) | Units 13-15 review | (111) | Unit 17 | (126) | Unit 19 |
| (97) | Units 13-15 review | (112) | Unit 17 | (127) | Unit 19 |
| (98) | Units 13-15 review | (113) | Unit 17 | (128) | Unit 19 |
| (99) | Units 13-15 review | (114) | Unit 17 practice | (129) | Unit 19 practice |
| (100) | Units 13-15 quiz | (115) | Unit 17 quiz | (130) | Unit 19 quiz |
| (101) | Units 1-3 review | (116) | Unit 18 | (131) | Unit 20 |
| (102) | Units 10-12 review | (117) | Unit 18 | (132) | Unit 20 |
| (103) | Units 4-6 review | (118) | Unit 18 | (133) | Unit 20 |
| (104) | Units 13-15 review | (119) | Unit 18 practice | (134) | Unit 20 practice |
| (105) | Units 7-9 review | (120) | Unit 18 quiz | (135) | Unit 20 quiz |

# Completion Chart for Lessons 136-170

| | | | | | |
|---|---|---|---|---|---|
| (136) | Unit 21 | (151) | Unit 23 | (166) | Units 16-18 review |
| (137) | Unit 21 | (152) | Unit 23 | (167) | Units 10-12 review |
| (138) | Unit 21 | (153) | Unit 23 | (168) | Units 1-3 review |
| (139) | Unit 21 practice | (154) | Unit 23 practice | (169) | Units 13-15 review |
| (140) | Unit 21 quiz | (155) | Unit 23 quiz | (170) | Units 4-6 review |
| (141) | Units 19-21 review | (156) | Unit 24 | | |
| (142) | Units 19-21 review | (157) | Unit 24 | | (No vocab for lessons 171-180) |
| (143) | Units 19-21 review | (158) | Unit 24 | | |
| (144) | Units 19-21 review | (159) | Unit 24 practice | | |
| (145) | Units 19-21 quiz | (160) | Unit 24 quiz | | |
| (146) | Unit 22 | (161) | Units 22-24 review | | |
| (147) | Unit 22 | (162) | Units 22-24 review | | |
| (148) | Unit 22 | (163) | Units 22-24 review | | |
| (149) | Unit 22 practice | (164) | Units 22-24 review | | |
| (150) | Unit 22 quiz | (165) | Units 22-24 quiz | | |

# Master Completion Chart

| Lesson | Reading | Vocabulary | LA | Lesson | Reading | Vocabulary | LA |
|---|---|---|---|---|---|---|---|
| 1 | ☐ | ☐ | ☐ | 42 | ☐ | ☐ | ☐ |
| 2 | ☐ | ☐ | ☐ | 43 | ☐ | ☐ | ☐ |
| 3 | ☐ | ☐ | ☐ | 44 | ☐ | ☐ | ☐ |
| 4 | ☐ | ☐ | ☐ | 45 | ☐ | ☐ | ☐ |
| 5 | ☐ | ☐ | ☐ | 46 | ☐ | ☐ | ☐ |
| 6 | ☐ | ☐ | ☐ | 47 | ☐ | ☐ | ☐ |
| 7 | ☐ | ☐ | ☐ | 48 | ☐ | ☐ | ☐ |
| 8 | ☐ | ☐ | ☐ | 49 | ☐ | ☐ | ☐ |
| 9 | ☐ | ☐ | ☐ | 50 | ☐ | ☐ | ☐ |
| 10 | ☐ | ☐ | ☐ | 51 | ☐ | ☐ | ☐ |
| 11 | ☐ | ☐ | ☐ | 52 | ☐ | ☐ | ☐ |
| 12 | ☐ | ☐ | ☐ | 53 | ☐ | ☐ | ☐ |
| 13 | ☐ | ☐ | ☐ | 54 | ☐ | ☐ | ☐ |
| 14 | ☐ | ☐ | ☐ | 55 | ☐ | ☐ | ☐ |
| 15 | ☐ | ☐ | ☐ | 56 | ☐ | ☐ | ☐ |
| 16 | ☐ | ☐ | ☐ | 57 | ☐ | ☐ | ☐ |
| 17 | ☐ | ☐ | ☐ | 58 | ☐ | ☐ | ☐ |
| 18 | ☐ | ☐ | ☐ | 59 | ☐ | ☐ | ☐ |
| 19 | ☐ | ☐ | ☐ | 60 | ☐ | ☐ | ☐ |
| 20 | ☐ | ☐ | ☐ | 61 | ☐ | ☐ | ☐ |
| 21 | ☐ | ☐ | ☐ | 62 | ☐ | ☐ | ☐ |
| 22 | ☐ | ☐ | ✗ | 63 | ✗ | ☐ | ☐ |
| 23 | ☐ | ☐ | ✗ | 64 | ✗ | ☐ | ☐ |
| 24 | ☐ | ☐ | ☐ | 65 | ✗ | ☐ | ☐ |
| 25 | ☐ | ☐ | ✗ | 66 | ✗ | ☐ | ☐ |
| 26 | ☐ | ☐ | ☐ | 67 | ☐ | ☐ | ✗ |
| 27 | ☐ | ☐ | ☐ | 68 | ☐ | ☐ | ☐ |
| 28 | ☐ | ☐ | ☐ | 69 | ☐ | ☐ | ☐ |
| 29 | ☐ | ☐ | ☐ | 70 | ☐ | ☐ | ☐ |
| 30 | ☐ | ☐ | ☐ | 71 | ☐ | ☐ | ☐ |
| 31 | ☐ | ☐ | ☐ | 72 | ☐ | ☐ | ☐ |
| 32 | ☐ | ☐ | ☐ | 73 | ☐ | ☐ | ☐ |
| 33 | ☐ | ☐ | ☐ | 74 | ☐ | ☐ | ☐ |
| 34 | ☐ | ☐ | ☐ | 75 | ☐ | ☐ | ☐ |
| 35 | ✗ | ☐ | ☐ | 76 | ☐ | ☐ | ☐ |
| 36 | ✗ | ☐ | ☐ | 77 | ☐ | ☐ | ☐ |
| 37 | ✗ | ☐ | ☐ | 78 | ☐ | ☐ | ☐ |
| 38 | ☐ | ☐ | ☐ | 79 | ☐ | ☐ | ✗ |
| 39 | ☐ | ☐ | ☐ | 80 | ☐ | ☐ | ☐ |
| 40 | ☐ | ☐ | ☐ | 81 | ☐ | ☐ | ☐ |
| 41 | ☐ | ☐ | ☐ | 82 | ☐ | ☐ | ☐ |

| Lesson | Reading | Vocabulary | LA | Lesson | Reading | Vocabulary | LA |
|---|---|---|---|---|---|---|---|
| 83 | ☐ | ☐ | ☐ | 126 | ☐ | ☐ | ☐ |
| 84 | ☐ | ☐ | ☐ | 127 | ☐ | ☐ | ☐ |
| 85 | ☐ | ☐ | ☐ | 128 | ☐ | ☐ | ☐ |
| 86 | ☐ | ☐ | ☐ | 129 | ☐ | ☐ | ☐ |
| 87 | ☐ | ☐ | ☐ | 130 | ☐ | ☐ | ☐ |
| 88 | ☐ | ☐ | ☐ | 131 | ☐ | ☐ | ☐ |
| 89 | ☐ | ☐ | ☐ | 132 | ☐ | ☐ | ☐ |
| 90 | ✕ | ☐ | ☐ | 133 | ☐ | ☐ | ✕ |
| 91 | ☐ | ☐ | ☐ | 134 | ☐ | ☐ | ✕ |
| 92 | ☐ | ☐ | ☐ | 135 | ☐ | ☐ | ✕ |
| 93 | ☐ | ☐ | ☐ | 136 | ☐ | ☐ | ✕ |
| 94 | ☐ | ☐ | ☐ | 137 | ☐ | ☐ | ✕ |
| 95 | ☐ | ☐ | ☐ | 138 | ☐ | ☐ | ✕ |
| 96 | ☐ | ☐ | ☐ | 139 | ☐ | ☐ | ✕ |
| 97 | ☐ | ☐ | ☐ | 140 | ☐ | ☐ | ✕ |
| 98 | ☐ | ☐ | ☐ | 141 | ☐ | ☐ | ✕ |
| 99 | ☐ | ☐ | ☐ | 142 | ☐ | ☐ | ☐ |
| 100 | ☐ | ☐ | ☐ | 143 | ☐ | ☐ | ✕ |
| 101 | ✕ | ☐ | ☐ | 144 | ☐ | ☐ | ✕ |
| 102 | ☐ | ☐ | ☐ | 145 | ☐ | ☐ | ✕ |
| 103 | ☐ | ☐ | ☐ | 146 | ☐ | ☐ | ☐ |
| 104 | ☐ | ☐ | ☐ | 147 | ☐ | ☐ | ✕ |
| 105 | ☐ | ☐ | ☐ | 148 | ☐ | ☐ | ✕ |
| 106 | ☐ | ☐ | ☐ | 149 | ☐ | ☐ | ✕ |
| 107 | ☐ | ☐ | ☐ | 150 | ☐ | ☐ | ✕ |
| 108 | ☐ | ☐ | ✕ | 151 | ☐ | ☐ | ✕ |
| 109 | ☐ | ☐ | ☐ | 152 | ☐ | ☐ | ☐ |
| 110 | ☐ | ☐ | ☐ | 153 | ☐ | ☐ | ☐ |
| 111 | ☐ | ☐ | ☐ | 154 | ☐ | ☐ | ☐ |
| 112 | ☐ | ☐ | ☐ | 155 | ☐ | ☐ | ☐ |
| 113 | ☐ | ☐ | ☐ | 156 | ☐ | ☐ | ☐ |
| 114 | ☐ | ☐ | ☐ | 157 | ☐ | ☐ | ☐ |
| 115 | ☐ | ☐ | ☐ | 158 | ☐ | ☐ | ☐ |
| 116 | ☐ | ☐ | ☐ | 159 | ☐ | ☐ | ☐ |
| 117 | ☐ | ☐ | ☐ | 160 | ☐ | ☐ | ☐ |
| 118 | ☐ | ☐ | ☐ | 161 | ☐ | ☐ | ☐ |
| 119 | ☐ | ☐ | ☐ | 162 | ☐ | ☐ | ☐ |
| 120 | ☐ | ☐ | ☐ | 163 | ☐ | ☐ | ☐ |
| 121 | ☐ | ☐ | ☐ | 164 | ☐ | ☐ | ☐ |
| 122 | ☐ | ☐ | ☐ | 165 | ☐ | ☐ | ☐ |
| 123 | ☐ | ☐ | ☐ | 166 | ☐ | ☐ | ☐ |
| 124 | ☐ | ☐ | ☐ | 167 | ☐ | ☐ | ✕ |
| 125 | ☐ | ☐ | ☐ | 168 | ☐ | ☐ | ✕ |

| Lesson | Reading | Vocabulary | LA |
|--------|---------|------------|-----|
| 169 | ☐ | ☐ | ☐ |
| 170 | ☐ | ☐ | ☐ |
| 171 | ☐ | ✕ | ✕ |
| 172 | ☐ | ✕ | ☐ |
| 173 | ☐ | ✕ | ☐ |
| 174 | ☐ | ✕ | ☐ |
| 175 | ☐ | ✕ | ☐ |
| 176 | ☐ | ✕ | ☐ |
| 177 | ☐ | ✕ | ☐ |
| 178 | ☐ | ✕ | ☐ |
| 179 | ☐ | ✕ | ☐ |
| 180 | ☐ | ✕ | ☐ |

# Lesson 1 Unit 1

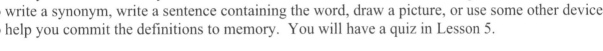

Here is your first vocabulary unit. Read each word and its definition. Use the space below each word to write a synonym, write a sentence containing the word, draw a picture, or use some other device to help you commit the definitions to memory. You will have a quiz in Lesson 5.

- **abbreviate** (v) reduce in scope while retaining essential elements; shorten

- **antagonize** (v) provoke the hostility of; act in opposition to

- **cacophony** (n) loud, confusing, disagreeable sounds

- **conflagration** (n) a very intense and uncontrolled fire; inferno

- **demeanor** (n) the way a person behaves toward other people

- **divert** (v) turn aside; send on a course or in a direction different from the planned or intended one

- **exemplary** (adj) worthy of imitation; being or serving as an illustration of a type; serving to warn

Continue learning your vocabulary unit. Read each word and its definition. Use the space below each word to write a synonym, write a sentence containing the word, draw a picture, or use some other device to help you commit the definitions to memory. You will have a quiz in Lesson 5.

- **fraudulent** (adj) intended to deceive

- **impassive** (adj) having or revealing little emotion or sensibility; not easily aroused or excited

- **insidious** (adj) beguiling but harmful; intended to entrap; working or spreading in a hidden and usually injurious way

- **longevity** (n) duration of service; the property of being long-lived

- **nascent** (adj) being born or beginning

- **oppose** (v) be against; contrast with equal weight or force; be resistant to

- **perspicacity** (n) intelligence manifested by being astute; the capacity to assess situations or circumstances shrewdly and to draw sound conclusions

Finish learning your vocabulary unit. Read each word and its definition. Use the space below each word to write a synonym, write a sentence containing the word, draw a picture, or use some other device to help you commit the definitions to memory. You will have a quiz in Lesson 5.

- **propensity** (n) an inclination to do something; a disposition to behave a certain way

- **reality** (n) the state of being actual or real; the state of the world as it really is rather than as you might want it to be

- **sacrosanct** (adj) must be kept sacred

- **submissive** (adj) inclined or willing to submit to orders or wishes of others

- **transient** (n) one who stays only a short time; (adj) of a mental act; causing effects outside the mind; lasting a very short time

- **veracity** (n) unwillingness to tell lies

# Lesson 4

Fill in the crossword puzzle with your vocabulary words. Study for your vocabulary quiz tomorrow. Make sure you know your words. Study ideas: read them out loud, copy the ones you are unsure of, have someone quiz you, use the words in conversation.

**Across:**
3. intelligence manifested by being astute
5. beginning
6. intended to entrap
8. must be kept sacred
13. a very intense and uncontrolled fire
15. one who stays only a short time
16. intended to deceive
18. worthy of imitation
19. willing to submit to orders or wishes of others

**Down:**
1. the way a person behaves toward others
2. not easily aroused or excited
3. a disposition to behave a certain way
4. loud, confusing, disagreeable sounds
7. turn aside
9. be against
10. unwillingness to tell lies
11. act in opposition to
12. duration of service
14. shorten
17. the state of being actual or real

You can study your words before you take this quiz, but you MUST put them away before you take the quiz. Cheaters get ZERO points for their quiz. Check your answers and record your score on your grade sheet (which can be printed online or found in the Language Arts workbook).

Circle the letter that contains the word that *best* fits.

1. The _____ of animal noises gave me a headache.

      a. cacophony      b. longevity      c. demeanor      d. veracity

2. His _____ behavior earned him the respect of the squad.

      a. fraudulent      b. insidious      c. exemplary      d. sacrosanct

3. The trench was dug to _____ the water away from the house.

      a. antagonize      b. oppose      c. abbreviate      d. divert

4. We had to _____ our lesson due to so many interruptions.

      a. oppose      b. abbreviate      c. antagonize      d. nascent

5. A synonym for inferno.

      a. transient      b. conflagration      c. demeanor      d. reality

Fill in the blank with the word that *best* fits.

6. The state of being actual or real is known as _____.

7. Something intended to deceive is _____.

8. An unwillingness to tell lies is _____.

9. Someone's _____ is the way they behave toward others.

10. A disposition to behave a certain way is a(n) _____.

Here is your next vocabulary unit. Read each word and its definition. Use the space below each word to write a synonym, write a sentence containing the word, draw a picture, or use some other device to help you commit the definitions to memory.  You will have a quiz in Lesson 10.

- **abstract** (adj) existing only in the mind; (n) a sketchy summary of the main points of a theory

- **anticipate** (v) regard something as probable or likely; be excited or anxious about

- **calumny** (n) a false accusation of an offense or a malicious misrepresentation of someone's words or actions

- **conformist** (n) someone who adheres to established standards of conduct; (adj) marked by convention and adherence to customs or rules; adhering to doctrines

- **demure** (adj) affectedly modest or shy, especially in a playful or provocative way

- **docile** (adj) willing to be taught or led; easily handled or managed

- **exigent** (adj) demanding attention; requiring precise accuracy

# Lesson 7 Unit 2

Continue learning your vocabulary unit. Read each word and its definition. Use the space below each word to write a synonym, write a sentence containing the word, draw a picture, or use some other device to help you commit the definitions to memory. You will have a quiz in Lesson 10.

- **frippery** (n) something of little value or significance

- **impervious** (adj) not admitting of passage or capable of being affected

- **integrity** (n) an undivided or unbroken completeness or totality with nothing wanting; moral soundness

- **loquacious** (adj) full of trivial conversation

- **nautical** (adj) relating to ships, navigation, or seamen

- **opulent** (adj) ostentatiously rich and superior in quality

- **pertinacious** (adj) stubbornly unyielding

# Lesson 8 Unit 2

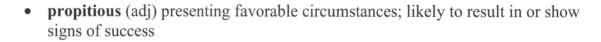

Finish learning your vocabulary unit. Read each word and its definition. Use the space below each word to write a synonym, write a sentence containing the word, draw a picture, or use some other device to help you commit the definitions to memory. You will have a quiz in Lesson 10.

- **propitious** (adj) presenting favorable circumstances; likely to result in or show signs of success

- **rebuke** (n) an act or expression of criticism and censure; (v) censure severely or angrily

- **sagacious** (adj) acutely insightful and wise; skillful in management

- **subordinate** (n) one subject to the control of another; (v) rank or order as less important; (adj) lower in rank or importance

- **translucent** (adj) allowing light to pass through diffusely

- **verdant** (adj) characterized by an abundance of lush green vegetation

# Lesson 9

Unit 2 Practice

Find your vocabulary words in the word search. As you find each one, repeat its definition. Look it up if you can't remember it. Study for your vocabulary quiz tomorrow. Make sure you know your words. Study ideas: read them out loud, copy the ones you are unsure of, have someone quiz you, use the words in conversation.

```
M T L F Y Y E I M D E O A N S C V U F P W
N H Q G S I T D V A E E C P F E G X X V L
B A Y G U E X I M E T M E A L X S P F E P
T P U Y S Y O R R S R R U S Q H U A J U K
A K L T T Y U X I G T D S R J K O P S W B
T S K R I S H M G I E U A N E R I Q W Z R
T N X C W C R A N R L T Z N E T V B Z E I
P M E R I O A A B U A S N I T R R A N T F
U Z L G F D C L K S U S A I P A E W R A W
Z A M N I I B Y A O T I C E U N P E W P R
Y R O L O X M K I F I R Q G D S M W J I I
D C U U M R E T R L Z S A O H L I B J C P
F O S K Y E I B V E W I C C V U S C T I A
R C M F U P K N X Z B I P L T C T O F T S
I X B T O F L W S X L U Z J Z E X X Z N B
P Z E R F A A D P E M T K V Z N S B C A E
P O P O P U L E N T D N O E I T D F I P M
E I O E O O T C A L U M N Y I P X I Z V H
R X M R W B P S U O I C A U Q O L P L S U
Y F E S A G A C I O U S W P K E F R M J A
Z S U B O R D I N A T E J I Z O P X S D S
```

| | | | |
|---|---|---|---|
| abstract | docile | loquacious | rebuke |
| anticipate | exigent | nautical | sagacious |
| calumny | frippery | opulent | subordinate |
| conformist | impervious | pertinacious | translucent |
| demure | integrity | propitious | verdant |

# Lesson 10                                    Unit 2 Quiz

You can study your words before you take this quiz, but you MUST put them away before you take the quiz. Cheaters get ZERO points for their quiz. Check your answers and record your score on your grade sheet.

Circle the letter that contains the word that *best* fits.

1. Sometimes quiet people become quite _____ when they're nervous.

    a. nautical    b. loquacious    c. abstract    d. translucent

2. The _____ businessman closed the deal.

    a. sagacious    b. verdant    c. abstract    d. exigent

3. Skipping the _____ , the couple bought a new home instead of having a showy wedding.

    a. calumny    b. integrity    c. frippery    d. rebuke

4. He loves to read under the _____ pines.

    a. verdant    b. conformist    c. impervious    d. nautical

5. A synonym for shy.

    a. docile    b. rebuke    c. demure    d. integrity

Fill in the blank with the word that *best* fits.

6. Something that exists only in the mind is known as _____.

7. Someone who adheres to established standards of conduct is a(n) _____.

8. Something that is _____ allows light to pass through diffusely.

9. Ostentatiously rich and superior in quality: _____.

10. An expression of criticism is a(n) _____.

# Lesson 11 Unit 3

Here is your next vocabulary unit. Read each word and its definition. Use the space below each word to write a synonym, write a sentence containing the word, draw a picture, or use some other device to help you commit the definitions to memory. You will have a quiz in Lesson 15.

- **acerbic** (adj) sour or bitter in taste; harsh or corrosive in tone

- **antipathy** (n) a feeling of intense dislike

- **camaraderie** (n) the quality of affording easy familiarity and sociability; friendship

- **congregation** (n) a group of people who adhere to a common faith; an assemblage of people or things collected together

- **depict** (v) show in a picture; give a description of; make a portrait of

- **ebullient** (adj) joyously unrestrained

- **expedite** (v) speed up the progress of; process fast and efficiently

Continue learning your vocabulary unit. Read each word and its definition. Use the space below each word to write a synonym, write a sentence containing the word, draw a picture, or use some other device to help you commit the definitions to memory.  You will have a quiz in Lesson 15.

- **fuse** (n) an electrical device that can interrupt the flow of current when overloaded; (v) mix together different elements

- **impetuous** (adj) characterized by undue haste and lack of thought or deliberation; marked by violent force

- **intransigent** (adj) impervious to pleas, persuasion, requests, reason

- **lucrative** (adj) producing a sizeable profit

- **negligent** (adj) characterized by neglect and undue lack of concern

- **orator** (n) a person who delivers a speech

- **petulance** (n) an irritable feeling

# Lesson 13          Unit 3

Finish learning your vocabulary unit. Read each word and its definition. Use the space below each word to write a synonym, write a sentence containing the word, draw a picture, or use some other device to help you commit the definitions to memory. You will have a quiz in Lesson 15.

- **prosaic** (adj) not fanciful or imaginative; lacking wit

- **recalcitrant** (adj) stubbornly resistant to authority or control

- **sagacity** (n) the mental ability to understand and discriminate between relations; the trait of forming opinions by distinguishing and evaluating

- **substantiate** (v) establish or strengthen as with new evidence or facts; represent in bodily form; make real or concrete

- **transmute** (v) change in outward structure or looks; alter the nature of (elements)

- **vex** (v) cause annoyance in; disturb; change the arrangement or position of; be a mystery

# Lesson 14

Unscramble your vocabulary words. Study for your vocabulary quiz tomorrow. Make sure you know your words. Study ideas: read them out loud, copy the ones you are unsure of, have someone quiz you, use the words in conversation.

**F S E U** _____

an electrical device that can interrupt the flow of current when overloaded

**G A I A Y T S C** _____

the trait of forming opinions by distinguishing and evaluating

**S T E U A S T A I N T B** _____

establish or strengthen as with new evidence or facts

**T L E L I N E U B** _____

joyously unrestrained

**D R A M C E I A E A R** _____

the quality of affording easy familiarity and sociability

**R O A O T R** _____

a person who delivers a speech

**N L N I G T G E E** _____

characterized by neglect and undue lack of concern

**M P O U U S I E T** _____

marked by violent force

**S N R T A T U M E** _____

change in outward structure or looks; alter the nature of (elements)

(continued on the next page)

T I R C E N T R L A C A    _____

stubbornly resistant to authority or control

C O I S P A R    _____

not fanciful or imaginative; lacking wit

G T N N T A I I E R S N    _____

impervious to pleas, persuasion, requests, reason

C T E D I P    _____

show in a picture; give a description of; make a portrait of

E X V    _____

cause annoyance in; disturb

A N G N O O I R G E C T    _____

an assemblage of people or things collected together

E I P D E E X T    _____

speed up the progress of; process fast and efficiently

A C I C E R B    _____

sour or bitter in taste; harsh or corrosive in tone

P T A A T N H Y I    _____

a feeling of intense dislike

A V I R L T E C U    _____

producing a sizeable profit

E U T P C N L E A    _____

an irritable feeling

You can study your words before you take this quiz, but you MUST put them away before you take the quiz. Cheaters get ZERO points for their quiz. Check your answers and record your score on your grade sheet.

Circle the letter that contains the word that *best* fits.

1.  The _____ between a boy and his dog is unparalleled.

    a. congregation      b. fuse      c. orator      d. camaraderie

2.  Our _____ lives have made us forget how to appreciate art.

    a. prosaic      b. recalcitrant      c. intransigent      d. lucrative

3.  The _____ delivered the speech with professionalism.

    a. sagacity      b. orator      c. antipathy      d. petulance

4.  The _____ song made her dance in her chair.

    a. acerbic      b. intransigent      c. recalcitrant      d. ebullient

5.  A synonym for annoy.

    a. vex      b. transmute      c. depict      d. expedite

Fill in the blank with the word that *best* fits.

6.  A synonym for sour: _____.

7.  To show in picture is to _____.

8.  Being characterized by undue haste and lack of thought is being _____.

9.  A feeling of intense dislike is _____.

10. Something producing a sizeable profit is _____.

# Lesson 16                    Units 1-3 Review

Look over all of your words and notes from the first three vocabulary units. Go over any rough spots in your memory.


# Lesson 17                    Units 1-3 Review

Find a partner to help you with this review game. See if you can guess the vocabulary word in ten guesses or less. Guess letters one at a time for each word and have your partner fill them in or let you know they're not in the word.


_ _ _ _ _ _ _ _ _ _          _ _ _ _ _ _ _

Hint: worthy of imitation              Hint: shy


_ _ _ _ _ _ _ _ _          _ _ _ _ _ _ _ _

Hint: easily handled              Hint: lacking wit


_ _ _ _ _ _ _ _ _ _          _ _ _ _ _ _ _ _

Hint: joyously unrestrained              Hint: turn aside


_ _ _ _ _ _ _ _ _ _          _ _ _ _ _ _ _ _

Hint: unwillingness to lie              Hint: censure severely


_ _ _ _ _ _ _ _          _ _ _ _ _

Hint: speed up the process              Hint: mix together

# Lesson 18

Match the word to its definition.

1. abbreviate       _____ a feeling of intense dislike

2. nascent          _____ demanding attention

3. sagacious        _____ must be kept sacred

4. antipathy        _____ false accusation of an offense

5. calumny          _____ ostentatiously rich and superior in quality

6. sagacity         _____ full of trivial conversation

7. intransigent     _____ beguiling but harmful

8. loquacious       _____ shorten

9. verdant          _____ sour or bitter in taste

10. acerbic         _____ acutely insightful and wise

11. substantiate    _____ one who stays only a short time

12. exigent         _____ beginning

13. perspicacity    _____ intelligence manifested by being astute

14. sacrosanct      _____ impervious to requests and reason

15. transient       _____ strengthen with new evidence

16. insidious       _____ ability to understand and discriminate between relations

17. opulent         _____ characterized by an abundance of lush green vegetation

# Lesson 19 — Units 1-3 Review

Can you find all 60 of your vocabulary words in this massive word search? Flip back through your three units for the word list if you need it.

```
N U S E S V J S V E R A C I T Y L Z Z V Q X J M C
A P T J L R Q O U B C V D C A C O P H O N Y W G O
U R M R L M G V G B B S U B O R D I N A T E C K N
T O E Q A O C D P N S P E R T I N A C I O U S N G
I P V N L N S Q S D Y T Q C F H G M W I T Z Y C R
C I E F O D S A E I J J A Y H R P C I S P G R A E
A T R R Q T A I C F N C A N E G L I G E N T S L G
L I D V U I B S E R X T L N T F H R Y B E Z A U A
L O A E A S B D N N O B R U T I R K E Z P U G M T
O U N X C A R O A D T S E A C I A I D A W F A N I
N S T F I G E C S E R P A X N R P T P V L Q C Y O
G J O Z O A V I C M A R K N T S A A E P P I I U N
E B E A U C I L E E N O D D C R I T T M E P T Y P
V V X C S I A E N A S S I E H T A G I H D R Y Y R
I P I E N O T O T N L A F P M A T N E V Y I Y Z O
T E M R R U E P P O U I U I W U R K S N E O I I P
Y T P B E S L P F R C C S C V X R D F M T R C N E
R U A I B H T O R H E B E T O I Y E A P U A X T N
B L S C U I L S L H N A N T I C I P A T E T V E S
P A S V K F Y E X A T Z J O P U L E N T J O E G I
E N I E E N I M P E R V I O U S L G M V R R J R T
B C V C A M A R A D E R I E E X E M P L A R Y I Y
U E E L I K G T W B F R A U D U L E N T Q C S T A
L J F D I V E R T Y K C O N F O R M I S T F H Y J
L T Y L Y V G J X Y C B G E X P E D I T E C E F V
I X I I N S I D I O U S L R A N T A G O N I Z E
E A W S U B M I S S I V E P E R S P I C A C I T Y
N C M T C B F A B S T R A C T K Z B K F L Q X E S
T C O N F L A G R A T I O N U I M P E T U O U S Y
E X I G E N T R E C A L C I T R A N T S A P G Y X
```

# Lesson 20

Units 1-3 Review Quiz

If you got 100% on all three of your vocabulary quizzes so far, no vocab for you today. Way to go! If you didn't, take this review quiz. If you score higher on this than you did on one of your previous quizzes, you may replace the grade of one of those quizzes on your grade sheet (just one).

Circle the letter that contains the word that *best* fits.

1.  Don't _____ your sister; get along!

    a. anticipate      b. antagonize      c. depict      d. transmute

2.  The clerk wouldn't cash the _____ check.

    a. impassive      b. pertinacious      c. recalcitrant      d. fraudulent

3.  A synonym for annoy.

    a. transmute      b. vex      c. anticipate      d. oppose

4.  An antonym of concrete.

    a. abstract      b. impassive      c. submissive      d. propitious

5.  The _____ teenager gets into trouble often.

    a. lucrative      b. nautical      c. recalcitrant      d. impassive

Fill in the blank with the word that *best* fits.

6.  Something relating to ships or navigation is known as _____.

7.  Not capable of being affected by something is being _____.

8.  An inclination to do something is a(n) _____.

9.  Stubbornly unyielding: _____.

10.  To be characterized by neglect and undue lack of concern is to be _____.

# Lesson 21                                                        Unit 4

Here is your next vocabulary unit. Read each word and its definition. Use the space below each word to write a synonym, write a sentence containing the word, draw a picture, or use some other device to help you commit the definitions to memory.  You will have a quiz in Lesson 25.

- **acumen** (n) shrewdness shown by keen insight

- **approbation** (n) official approval

- **capricious** (adj) changeable; determined by chance or impulse or whim rather than by necessity or reason

- **connotation** (n) what you must know in order to determine the reference of an expression; an idea that is implied or suggested

- **deprecate** (v) belittle; express strong disapproval of

- **eclipse** (n) one celestial body obscures another; (v) be greater in significance than

- **expiate** (v) make amends for

Continue learning your vocabulary unit. Read each word and its definition. Use the space below each word to write a synonym, write a sentence containing the word, draw a picture, or use some other device to help you commit the definitions to memory.  You will have a quiz in Lesson 25.

- **garrulous** (adj) full of trivial conversation

- **impinge** (v) infringe upon; advance beyond the usual limit

- **intrepid** (adj) invulnerable to fear or intimidation

- **maelstrom** (n) a powerful circular current of water (usually the result of conflicting tides)

- **neophyte** (n) a new participant in some activity; someone young or inexperienced

- **orient** (n) the hemisphere that includes Eurasia, Africa, and Australia; (v) point; determine one's position with reference to another point; cause to point

- **pious** (adj) having or showing or expressing reverence for a deity

# Lesson 23                                    Unit 4

Finish learning your vocabulary unit. Read each word and its definition. Use the space below each word to write a synonym, write a sentence containing the word, draw a picture, or use some other device to help you commit the definitions to memory. You will have a quiz in Lesson 25.

- **proscribe** (v) command against

- **reclusive** (adj) withdrawn from society; seeking solitude; providing privacy or seclusion

- **sanctimonious** (adj) excessively or hypocritically pious

- **subtle** (adj) difficult to detect or grasp; able to make fine distinctions; working or spreading in a hidden and usually injurious way

- **trenchant** (adj) having keenness and forcefulness in thought, expression, or intellect; characterized by force and vigor; clearly or sharply defined to the mind

- **vicarious** (adj) experienced at secondhand

# Lesson 24

## Unit 4 Practice

Fill in the crossword puzzle with your vocabulary words. Study for your vocabulary quiz tomorrow. Make sure you know your words. Study ideas: read them out loud, copy the ones you are unsure of, have someone quiz you, use the words in conversation.

**Across:**
3. make amends for
6. full of trivial conversation
7. showing reverence for a deity
9. clearly or sharply defined to the mind
14. express strong disapproval of
17. excessively or hypocritically pious
19. be greater in significance than
20. a powerful circular current of water

**Down:**
1. infringe upon
2. shrewdness shown by keen insight
4. official approval
5. difficult to detect or grasp
8. invulnerable to fear or intimidation
10. changeable
11. experienced at secondhand
12. someone young or inexperienced
13. withdrawn from society
15. an idea that is implied or suggested
16. command against
18. point

# Lesson 25 Unit 4 Quiz

You can study your words before you take this quiz, but you MUST put them away before you take the quiz. Cheaters get ZERO points for their quiz. Check your answers and record your score on your grade sheet.

Circle the letter that contains the word that *best* fits.

1. Her business _____ was unparalleled.

   a. connotation    b. eclipse        c. acumen         d. maelstrom

2. We couldn't believe it when our _____ friend auditioned for the musical.

   a. reclusive      b. trenchant      c. vicarious      d. capricious

3. The powerful _____ brought down the ship.

   a. eclipse        b. maelstrom      c. approbation    d. orient

4. His _____ attempt at humor was lost on me.

   a. vicarious      b. reclusive      c. intrepid       d. subtle

5. To command against.

   a. impinge        b. proscribe      c. expiate        d. deprecate

Fill in the blank with the word that *best* fits.

6. An official approval is a(n) _____.

7. To belittle is to _____.

8. When you advance beyond the usual limit, you _____.

9. To determine your position relative to another point is to _____.

10. Experienced at secondhand: _____.

Here is your next vocabulary unit. Read each word and its definition. Use the space below each word to write a synonym, write a sentence containing the word, draw a picture, or use some other device to help you commit the definitions to memory. You will have a quiz in Lesson 30.

- **adhere** (v) follow through or carry out a plan; stick to firmly

- **arrogate** (v) demand as being one's due or property; assert one's right to; take without authority

- **censure** (n) harsh criticism or disapproval; (v) rebuke formally

- **consecutive** (adj) one after the other; successive without a break; (adv) in a manner that is successive

- **derogatory** (adj) expressive of low opinion

- **effrontery** (n) audacious behavior that you have no right to

- **exploit** (n) a notable achievement; (v) use or manipulate to one's advantage; draw from; make good use of; work excessively hard

# Lesson 27                                    Unit 5

Continue learning your vocabulary unit. Read each word and its definition. Use the space below each word to write a synonym, write a sentence containing the word, draw a picture, or use some other device to help you commit the definitions to memory. You will have a quiz in Lesson 30.

- **generalize** (v) draw from specific cases for more general cases; bring into general or common use

- **implacable** (adj) incapable of being placated or appeased

- **intuitive** (adj) spontaneously derived from or prompted by a natural tendency; obtained through intuition rather than from reasoning or observation

- **malediction** (n) a curse

- **nonchalant** (adj) marked by blithe unconcern

- **ostensible** (adj) appearing as such but not necessarily so; pretended

- **pithy** (adj) concise and full of meaning

Finish learning your vocabulary unit. Read each word and its definition. Use the space below each word to write a synonym, write a sentence containing the word, draw a picture, or use some other device to help you commit the definitions to memory.  You will have a quiz in Lesson 30.

- **prosperity** (n) an economic state of growth with rising profits and full employment; having good fortune

- **reconciliation** (n) the reestablishing of cordial relations; getting two things to correspond

- **sanction** (n) formal and explicit approval; (v) give permission to

- **succor** (n) assistance in time of difficulty; (v) help in a difficult situation

- **trilateral** (n) a three-sided polygon; (adj) involving three parties; having three sides

- **vicissitude** (n) a variation in circumstances or fortune at different times in your life or in the development of something

# Lesson 29

Unit 5 Practice

Find your vocabulary words in the word search. As you find each one, repeat its definition. Look it up if you can't remember it. Study for your vocabulary quiz tomorrow. Make sure you know your words. Study ideas: read them out loud, copy the ones you are unsure of, have someone quiz you, use the words in conversation.

```
L  P  T  A  N  I  M  P  L  A  C  A  B  L  E  U  G  O  N  P  D  W
A  Y  V  N  Q  S  F  S  A  N  I  W  R  Q  Z  P  D  X  D  T  N  A
D  G  S  F  C  B  Y  J  N  J  A  M  G  V  I  L  G  Y  Z  K  X  I
E  L  U  T  P  C  B  W  F  I  T  B  L  M  V  B  T  D  B  Q  Q  S
R  C  C  T  Y  I  K  T  D  J  Y  P  B  M  E  I  H  V  T  X  C  V
O  R  C  J  Y  J  T  L  R  J  F  E  W  G  R  I  I  N  Y  Y  E  A
G  L  O  P  H  U  D  H  T  G  V  J  C  E  L  K  A  N  R  E  N  D
A  C  R  V  U  U  W  A  Y  I  Z  E  P  A  O  L  E  E  T  B  S  H
T  B  Q  T  U  C  H  N  T  C  L  S  R  U  A  N  T  A  K  E  U  E
O  N  E  L  S  L  O  U  L  B  O  E  E  H  O  N  G  L  Q  N  R  R
R  T  L  M  J  I  C  P  I  R  T  D  C  I  O  O  S  E  Z  Q  E  E
Y  I  Y  N  T  E  T  S  P  A  U  N  T  R  R  X  O  K  I  S  X  G
P  A  V  C  S  S  N  S  L  T  O  C  F  R  F  B  J  Y  Z  Y  Q  Z
W  D  N  N  G  E  W  I  I  N  I  F  A  O  U  Z  Z  N  E  D  H  X
D  A  O  Q  T  Y  R  S  X  D  E  J  E  X  P  L  O  I  T  B  R  I
S  C  U  S  E  T  S  U  E  P  R  C  A  E  P  T  M  O  S  W  F  W
B  R  O  M  H  I  T  L  L  K  F  F  A  U  Z  O  C  T  Q  I  E  N
D  O  D  W  C  G  A  G  W  G  E  N  E  R  A  L  I  Z  E  I  N  B
K  L  P  I  X  M  S  G  X  K  C  D  H  M  S  K  U  I  C  G  L  C
N  S  V  K  D  J  C  F  F  F  U  G  P  K  X  Y  D  Q  U  F  S  Y
H  Y  G  I  K  T  F  O  R  I  I  N  T  U  I  T  I  V  E  L  S  E
R  E  C  O  N  C  I  L  I  A  T  I  O  N  B  W  N  V  U  O  F  H
```

| | | | |
|---|---|---|---|
| adhere | effrontery | malediction | reconciliation |
| arrogate | exploit | nonchalant | sanction |
| censure | generalize | ostensible | succor |
| consecutive | implacable | pithy | trilateral |
| derogatory | intuitive | prosperity | vicissitude |

# Lesson 30                                     Unit 5 Quiz

You can study your words before you take this quiz, but you MUST put them away before you take the quiz. Cheaters get ZERO points for their quiz. Check your answers and record your score on your grade sheet.

Circle the letter that contains the word that *best* fits.

1. You need to strictly _____ to the rules to be a member at that club.

    a. arrogate    b. generalize    c. exploit    d. adhere

2. The soldier was sent home after receiving another _____ from his superior officer.

    a. effrontery    b. censure    c. malediction    d. prosperity

3. The Red Cross provided _____ after the hurricane.

    a. reconciliation    b. vicissitude    c. censure    d. succor

4. The _____ book title told me all I needed to know.

    a. pithy    b. consecutive    c. implacable    d. nonchalant

5. We received _____ to proceed with the plan.

    a. prosperity    b. sanction    c. malediction    d. exploit

Fill in the blank with the word that *best* fits.

6. A curse: _____.

7. A notable achievement: _____.

8. Something that is _____ is expressive of low opinion.

9. A three-sided polygon is a(n) _____.

10. One after the other is known as _____.

Here is your next vocabulary unit. Read each word and its definition. Use the space below each word to write a synonym, write a sentence containing the word, draw a picture, or use some other device to help you commit the definitions to memory.  You will have a quiz in Lesson 35.

- **adulation** (n) exaggerated and hypocritical praise

- **ascetic** (n) someone who practices self-denial as a spiritual discipline; (adj) practicing great self-denial

- **characteristic** (n) a prominent attribute or aspect of something; a distinguishing quality; (adj) typical or distinctive

- **constituent** (n) a citizen who is represented in a government by officials for whom he or she votes; something determined in relation to something that includes it

- **desecrate** (v) violate the sacred character of a place or language; remove the consecration from a person or an object

- **egocentric** (n) a self-centered person with little regard for others; (adj) limited to or caring only about yourself and your own needs

- **expunge** (v) remove by erasing or crossing out or as if by drawing a line

# Lesson 32 Unit 6

Continue learning your vocabulary unit. Read each word and its definition. Use the space below each word to write a synonym, write a sentence containing the word, draw a picture, or use some other device to help you commit the definitions to memory. You will have a quiz in Lesson 35.

- **glaring** (v) looking at with a fixed glaze; shining intensely; (adj) shining intensely; conspicuously and outrageously bad or reprehensible

- **impudent** (adj) marked by casual disrespect; improperly forward or bold

- **inure** (v) cause to accept or become hardened to; habituate

- **malleable** (adj) easily influenced; capable of being shaped or bent or drawn out

- **nostalgia** (n) longing for something past

- **ostentatious** (adj) intended to attract notice and impress others; tawdry or vulgar

- **platitude** (n) a trite or obvious remark

# Lesson 33 Unit 6

Finish learning your vocabulary unit. Read each word and its definition. Use the space below each word to write a synonym, write a sentence containing the word, draw a picture, or use some other device to help you commit the definitions to memory. You will have a quiz in Lesson 35.

- **protean** (adj) taking on different forms

- **rectitude** (n) righteousness as a consequence of being honorable and honest

- **sanguine** (n) a blood-red color; (adj) confidently optimistic and cheerful

- **superficial** (adj) concerned with or comprehending only what is apparent or obvious; not deep or penetrating emotionally or intellectually; being near the surface; hasty and without attention to detail

- **truculent** (adj) defiantly aggressive

- **vilify** (v) spread negative information about

# Lesson 34

Unscramble your vocabulary words. Study for your vocabulary quiz tomorrow. Make sure you know your words. Study ideas: read them out loud, copy the ones you are unsure of, have someone quiz you, use the words in conversation.

E T R C D E S A E

violate the sacred character of a place or language

_____

U T S O N N T T I C E

a citizen who is represented in a government by officials for whom he or she votes

_____

L U I T E D T P A

a trite or obvious remark

_____

E C I C S T A

someone who practices self-denial as a spiritual discipline

_____

A S H E R C C R I A T C I T

typical or distinctive

_____

C E R I T C E G N O

a self-centered person with little regard for others

_____

I V I Y L F

spread negative information about

_____

U N N E A S I G

confidently optimistic and cheerful

_____

O T N L A U A D I

exaggerated and hypocritical praise

_____

(continued on the next page)

T A A L O I S N G                          _____

longing for something past

X U G E N E P                              _____

remove by erasing or crossing out or as if by drawing a line

E T P N U D M I                            _____

marked by casual disrespect; improperly forward or bold

F L R I I P U E S C A                      _____

concerned with or comprehending only what is apparent or obvious

R P O A N T E                              _____

taking on different forms

G I G N A L R                              _____

looking at with a fixed glaze; shining intensely

A L E A L M L E B                          _____

capable of being shaped or bent or drawn out

E T U C D R I T E                          _____

righteousness as a consequence of being honorable and honest

T U C L E N T R U                          _____

defiantly aggressive

I T T N A T O E U S O S                    _____

intended to attract notice and impress others

N E I R U                                  _____

cause to accept or become hardened to

You can study your words before you take this quiz, but you MUST put them away before you take the quiz. Cheaters get ZERO points for their quiz. Check your answers and record your score on your grade sheet.

Circle the letter that contains the word that *best* fits.

1.  My brother was _____ at me when I used his computer without asking.

     a. protean     b. ostentatious     c. impudent     d. glaring

2.  Flying is _____ of flies.

     a. ascetic     b. characteristic     c. truculent     d. malleable

3.  The _____ girl had trouble making friends.

     a. egocentric     b. inure     c. ostentatious     d. sanguine

4. Certain smells take me back to my childhood and make me feel strong _____.

     a. rectitude     b. ascetic     c. nostalgia     d. adulation

5.  A synonym for habituate.

     a. inure     b. desecrate     c. expunge     d. glaring

Fill in the blank with the word that *best* fits.

6.  Exaggerated and hypocritical praise is _____.

7.  Capable of being shaped is known as _____.

8.  Intended to attract notice and impress others: _____.

9.  Taking on different forms is known as _____.

10.  A trite or obvious remark is a(n) _____.

# Lesson 36 Units 4-6 Review

Look over all of your words and notes from the past three vocabulary units (4-6). Go over any rough spots in your memory.

# Lesson 37 Units 4-6 Review

Find a partner to help you with this review game. See if you can guess the vocabulary word in ten guesses or less. Guess letters one at a time for each word and have your partner fill them in or let you know they're not in the word.

— — — — — — — — — —

Hint: exaggerated praise

— — — — — — — —

Hint: point

— — — — — — — —

Hint: keen insight

— — — — — — — — —

Hint: notable achievement

— — — — — — — — — — —

Hint: violate sacred character

— — — — — — —

Hint: full of meaning

— — — — — — — — — —

Hint: invulnerable to fear

— — — — — — — —

Hint: help during difficult times

— — — — — — — — —

Hint: assert one's right to

— — — — — —

Hint: habituate

# Lesson 38

Match the word to its definition.

1. approbation    _____ taking on different forms

2. ostensible    _____ changeable

3. ascetic    _____ a curse

4. protean    _____ self-centered

5. derogatory    _____ capable of being shaped or bent

6. garrulous    _____ pretended

7. capricious    _____ longing for something past

8. adhere    _____ defiantly aggressive

9. egocentric    _____ official approval

10. truculent    _____ withdrawn from society

11. malediction    _____ expressive of low opinion

12. impudent    _____ incapable of being pleased

13. malleable    _____ stick to firmly

14. implacable    _____ give permission to

15. reclusive    _____ full of trivial conversation

16. sanction    _____ marked by casual disrespect

17. nostalgia    _____ practicing great self-denial

# Lesson 39

Units 4-6 Review

Can you find all 60 of your vocabulary words in this massive word search? Flip back through the three units for the word list if you need it.

```
P D E A Y Z N O S D O N S I P Z A B E I O A I E J Y P E Z H
R J E U Q G O S U E S V X G Y L J K Y M G H N G D C E X O K
Q Q G I U E S T B S T Q H V E E A N I H O U T O H B K P L E
O Z U G I J T E T E E I E A X N F T V O K H R C F C F U X Y
X J B H T U A N L C N M X P P P E T I R C E E E D A A N H V
U A P C A B L S E R T P E P L R F R R T M K P N Y A R G A I
A M F G B W G I T A A U C R O E C Z A E U R I T B M R E D C
D A H L Z K I B C T T D L O I Z G H D L N D D R I N O S U A
H L T A C O A L Y E I E I B T Q A Q A P I C E I W W G N L R
E L R R O K D E G J O N P A U F W B G R R Z H C V R A O A I
R E I I N S P E A D U T S T Y P W I R C A O E A S T T N T O
E A L N N V I E X I S K E I A N R F N C B C T W N P E C I U
T B A G O S O F S W N R P O G T M O E T I S T E H T N H O S
P L T S T U U F A W M U L N E H U N S H U G G E A H T A N V
R E E A A P S R N V B B R Z R G Q E Q P V I A S R N R L F I
O D R N T E N O C C I M P E E G N O X I E W T R U I D A B L
S P A C I R A N T O P C M B C Z J P D A M R E I R C S N T I
C W L T O F U T I N R G I C L C M H B Y W P I H V U C T N F
R D P I N I M E O S E P L S U C C Y T J W C I T S E L O I Y
I E I M N C A R N E X F H W S D C T W D G E B N Y H C O R C
B P T O G I E Y A C P T C C I I E E X H L N Y K G U O Z U Y
E R H N M A L W C U I Q B A V C T R B G V S A D O E N P R S
O E Y I V L S E U T A Q M P E S X U O B N U X B R T S I E T
O C R O X Z T K M I T F W R C B O N D G J R E D I O T C C G
W A K U I X R W E V E Z K I V D B R R E A E E A P I F T J
J T D S N B O L N E F G J C M A L E D I C T I O N F T O I P
D E D F N V M R E C O N C I L I A T I O N P O B T G U V T K
R L Y C Y A K R G B D A A O T R U C U L E N T R X X E S U O
P N I M P L A C A B L E H U H X F T L L J Y Q T Y U N Q D F
T V K P S A N G U I N E V S D A S C E T I C R F E B T A E T
```

# Lesson 40                                    Units 4-6 Review Quiz

If you got 100% on all three of your vocabulary quizzes so far, no vocab for you today. Way to go!
If you didn't, take this review quiz. If you score higher on this than you did on one of your previous
quizzes, you may replace the grade of one of those quizzes on your grade sheet (just one).

Circle the letter that contains the word that *best* fits.

1.  The politician created an ad to _____ his opponent.

    a. generalize       b. vilify        c. expiate        d. adhere

2.  The juror had the _____ to challenge the expert's opinion.

    a. effrontery       b. prosperity        c. constituent        d. connotation

3.  You should not _____ your own worth.

    a. expiate        b. deprecate        c. generalize        d. expunge

4.  The girl gave a _____ shrug.

    a. trilateral        b. sanctimonious        c. vicarious        d. nonchalant

5.  The fur coat was a bit _____ for the funeral.

    a. intuitive        b. consecutive        c. ostentatious        d. trenchant

Fill in the blank with the word that *best* fits.

6.  A new participant in an activity is a(n) _____.


7.  An idea that is implied or suggested is a(n) _____.


8.  To be greater in significance than is to _____.


9.  To be excessively or hypocritically pious is to be _____.


10.  Something involving three parties is known as _____.

# Lesson 41                                    Unit 7

Here is your next vocabulary unit. Read each word and its definition. Use the space below each word to write a synonym, write a sentence containing the word, draw a picture, or use some other device to help you commit the definitions to memory. You will have a quiz in Lesson 45.

- **adumbrate** (v) describe roughly or briefly

- **aspersion** (n) a disparaging remark; an abusive attack on a person's character

- **circuitous** (adj) deviating from a straight course; indirect

- **contingent** (n) a gathering of persons representative of some larger group; (adj) possible but not certain to occur; being determined by conditions that follow

- **desiccate** (v) preserve by removing all water and liquids from; lose water or moisture; (adj) lacking vitality or spirit; lifeless

- **egregious** (adj) conspicuously and outrageously bad or reprehensible

- **extant** (adj) still in existence; not extinct or destroyed or lost

# Lesson 42 Unit 7

Continue learning your vocabulary unit. Read each word and its definition. Use the space below each word to write a synonym, write a sentence containing the word, draw a picture, or use some other device to help you commit the definitions to memory. You will have a quiz in Lesson 45.

- **grandeur** (n) the quality of being magnificent or splendid; the quality of elevation of mind and exaltation of character or ideals or conduct

- **impute** (v) attribute or credit to; ascribe

- **invective** (n) abusive or venomous language used to express blame or censure or bitter deep-seated ill will

- **manifold** (n) a pipe that has several lateral outlets to or from other pipes (v) make multiple copies of; (adj) having many features or forms

- **notion** (n) a vague idea in which some confidence is placed; a general inclusive concept; a fanciful idea; small personal articles, clothing, or sewing items

- **palliate** (v) lessen or try to lessen the seriousness or extent of; provide physical relief, as from pain

- **plethora** (n) extreme excess

# Lesson 43                                          Unit 7

Finish learning your vocabulary unit. Read each word and its definition. Use the space below each word to write a synonym, write a sentence containing the word, draw a picture, or use some other device to help you commit the definitions to memory.  You will have a quiz in Lesson 45.

- **provocative** (adj) serving or tending to provoke, excite, or stimulate

- **redeem** (v) restore the honor or worth of; to turn in and receive something in exchange

- **scrutinize** (v) to look at critically or searchingly; examine carefully for accuracy

- **superfluous** (adj) serving no useful purpose; having no excuse for being; more than is needed, desired, or required

- **turgid** (adj) ostentatiously lofty in style; abnormally distended especially by fluids or gas

- **vindicate** (v) show to be right by providing justification or proof; maintain, uphold, or defend; clear of accusation

# Lesson 44

Fill in the crossword puzzle with your vocabulary words. Study for your vocabulary quiz tomorrow. Make sure you know your words. Study ideas: read them out loud, copy the ones you are unsure of, have someone quiz you, use the words in conversation.

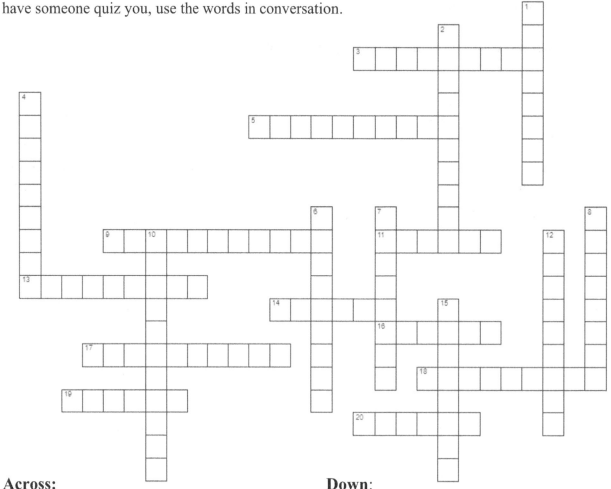

**Across:**

3. abusive language used to express blame
5. being determined by conditions that follow
9. serving no useful purpose
11. restore the honor or worth of
13. conspicuously, outrageously bad
14. ostentatiously lofty in style
16. still in existence
17. deviating from a straight course
18. maintain, uphold, or defend
19. attribute or credit to
20. a general inclusive concept

**Down:**

1. extreme excess
2. to look at critically or searchingly
4. preserve by removing all liquids from
6. a disparaging remark
7. the quality of being splendid
8. lessen or try to lessen the seriousness of
10. serving to provoke, excite, or stimulate
12. describe roughly or briefly
15. having many features or forms

# Lesson 45            Unit 7 Quiz

You can study your words before you take this quiz, but you MUST put them away before you take the quiz. Cheaters get ZERO points for their quiz. Check your answers and record your score on your grade sheet.

Circle the letter that contains the word that *best* fits.

1.  Repeated sun exposure tends to _____ the skin.

    a. adumbrate     b. impute     c. desiccate     d. palliate

2.  The _____ route left me disoriented.

    a. circuitous     b. egregious     c. provocative     d. turgid

3.  The _____ of shoes took over her closet.

    a. aspersion     b. plethora     c. grandeur     d. manifold

4. My mom will _____ my cleaning job much more closely than will my dad.

    a. scrutinize     b. impute     c. redeem     d. vindicate

5.  _____ errors were caused by my failure to spellcheck.

    a. Extant     b. Egregious     c. Turgid     d. Provocative

Fill in the blank with the word that *best* fits.

6.  To describe roughly or briefly is to _____.

7.  A disparaging remark is a(n) _____.

8.  To attribute credit to is to _____.

9.  Something serving no useful purpose can be descried as _____.

10.  The quality of being magnificent or splendid is known as _____.

# Lesson 46                                                                    Unit 8

Here is your next vocabulary unit. Read each word and its definition. Use the space below each word to write a synonym, write a sentence containing the word, draw a picture, or use some other device to help you commit the definitions to memory. You will have a quiz in Lesson 50.

- **adversity** (n) a state of misfortune or affliction; a calamitous event

- **assert** (v) state categorically; declare or affirm solemnly as true; insist on having one's opinions and rights recognized

- **circumvent** (v) surround so as to force to give up; avoid; beat through cleverness and wit

- **contradiction** (n) opposition between two conflicting forces or ideas; a statement that is necessarily false

- **devoid** (adj) completely wanting or lacking

- **elusive** (adj) difficult to describe; skillful at avoiding capture; difficult to detect or grasp by the mind

- **extemporaneous** (adj) with little or no preparation or forethought

# Lesson 47                                    Unit 8

Continue learning your vocabulary unit. Read each word and its definition. Use the space below each word to write a synonym, write a sentence containing the word, draw a picture, or use some other device to help you commit the definitions to memory.  You will have a quiz in Lesson 50.

- **grandiloquence** (n) high-flown style; excessive use of verbal ornamentation

- **inchoate** (adj) only partly in existence; imperfectly formed

- **inveterate** (adj) habitual; (adv) in a habitual and longstanding manner

- **marauder** (n) someone who attacks in search of booty

- **novice** (n) someone new to a field or activity; beginner

- **pallid** (adj) abnormally deficient in color as suggesting physical or emotional distress; dim or feeble; lacking in vitality or interest

- **polemic** (n) a writer who argues in opposition to others; a controversy; (adj) of or involving dispute or controversy

Finish learning your vocabulary unit. Read each word and its definition. Use the space below each word to write a synonym, write a sentence containing the word, draw a picture, or use some other device to help you commit the definitions to memory.  You will have a quiz in Lesson 50.

- **proximity** (n) the property of being close together; the region close around a person or thing

- **redundant** (adj) more than is needed, desired, or required; repetition of same sense in different words

- **scurrilous** (adj) expressing offensive reproach

- **surfeit** (n) the state of being more than full; the quality of being so overabundant that prices fall; (v) supply or feed to fullness

- **turpitude** (n) a corrupt or depraved act or practice

- **vindictive** (adj) disposed to seek revenge; showing malicious ill-will and a desire to hurt

# Lesson 49

Find your vocabulary words in the word search. As you find each one, repeat its definition. Look it up if you can't remember it. Study for your vocabulary quiz tomorrow. Make sure you know your words. Study ideas: read them out loud, copy the ones you are unsure of, have someone quiz you, use the words in conversation.

```
A  S  X  S  M  D  T  N  O  V  I  C  E  H  T  Q  R  C  E  J  O
N  M  T  U  R  P  I  T  U  D  E  B  K  N  F  T  X  M  X  G  E
D  F  K  Z  G  R  P  V  P  R  I  O  A  W  R  L  W  X  T  R  X
A  O  W  I  C  U  Z  D  F  V  P  D  D  E  Z  M  J  B  E  A  N
I  I  M  T  K  Q  I  H  Y  Q  N  I  S  Z  V  T  U  C  M  N  J
F  J  Q  T  E  L  Q  C  A  U  E  S  V  H  N  Y  O  P  P  D  A
P  V  M  M  L  X  N  K  D  X  A  Y  L  E  J  Z  P  R  O  I  G
K  Q  T  A  P  O  L  E  M  I  C  S  V  A  N  L  K  O  R  L  N
Z  B  P  H  M  M  R  Q  U  E  K  M  F  C  X  R  G  X  A  O  S
P  W  J  M  E  A  T  X  T  D  U  Y  X  G  A  O  P  I  N  Q  C
R  M  B  S  E  O  R  A  V  C  E  L  U  S  I  V  E  M  E  U  U
M  V  G  U  B  A  R  A  R  I  C  F  X  H  X  L  C  I  O  E  R
A  F  F  R  I  E  D  I  U  T  N  K  A  Y  S  D  N  T  U  N  R
X  K  D  F  T  N  C  V  F  D  O  D  I  Y  I  M  Q  Y  S  C  I
X  Q  H  E  U  N  C  K  E  J  E  L  I  O  L  F  Y  U  F  E  L
V  P  V  I  P  Y  T  H  R  R  W  R  V  C  R  K  Z  L  N  F  O
J  N  Z  T  R  G  N  D  O  P  S  E  S  C  T  R  F  P  F  C  U
I  O  U  B  T  B  P  E  I  A  D  I  M  W  Q  I  T  C  I  O  S
G  F  B  T  G  O  H  I  F  R  T  X  T  N  I  I  V  J  A  O  A
L  O  F  W  L  O  W  A  X  M  Z  E  B  Y  M  Y  R  E  R  D  O
V  Q  T  C  O  N  T  R  A  D  I  C  T  I  O  N  Q  G  O  Y  X
```

| | | | |
|---|---|---|---|
| adversity | elusive | marauder | redundant |
| assert | extemporaneous | novice | scurrilous |
| circumvent | grandiloquence | pallid | surfeit |
| contradiction | inchoate | polemic | turpitude |
| devoid | inveterate | proximity | vindictive |

You can study your words before you take this quiz, but you MUST put them away before you take the quiz. Cheaters get ZERO points for their quiz. Check your answers and record your score on your grade sheet.

Circle the letter that contains the word that *best* fits.

1.  Despite great _____, the team won the championship.

    a. grandiloquence     b. surfeit     c. adversity     d. turpitude

2.  The _____ squirrel dropped acorns on my car when I forgot to refill the feeder.

    a. vindictive     b. redundant     c. pallid     d. extemporaneous

3.  The speech was not supposed to be _____, but I forgot it was due today.

    a. pallid     b. extemporaneous     c. scurrilous     d. devoid

4.  After laying on it all night, my arm was _____ of all feeling.

    a. elusive     b. devoid     c. inchoate     d. polemic

5.  The article is a(n) _____ against those who are in power.

    a. polemic     b. adversity     c. marauder     d. surfeit

Fill in the blank with the word that *best* fits.

6.  Opposition between two conflicting forces is known as _____.

7.  To state categorically is to _____.

8.  Something only partly in existence is _____.

9.  A synonym for *habitual*: _____.

10. The state of being more than full is known as _____.

# Lesson 51                                          Unit 9

Here is your next vocabulary unit. Read each word and its definition. Use the space below each word to write a synonym, write a sentence containing the word, draw a picture, or use some other device to help you commit the definitions to memory. You will have a quiz in Lesson 55.

- **advocate** (n) a person who pleads for a cause; (v) push for something; argue in favor of

- **assiduous** (adj) marked by care and persistent effort

- **clairvoyant** (adj) perceiving things beyond the natural range of the senses

- **contrite** (adj) feeling or expressing pain or sorrow for sins or offenses

- **diaphanous** (adj) so thin as to transmit light; see-through

- **eminent** (adj) standing above others in quality or position; of imposing height

- **extenuating** (v) lessen or try to lessen the seriousness or extent of; (adj) partially excusing or justifying

Continue learning your vocabulary unit. Read each word and its definition. Use the space below each word to write a synonym, write a sentence containing the word, draw a picture, or use some other device to help you commit the definitions to memory. You will have a quiz in Lesson 55.

- **gregarious** (adj) instinctively or temperamentally seeking and enjoying the company of others; plants growing in groups that are close together; animals tending to form a group with others of the same species

- **incompatible** (adj) not easy to combine harmoniously; not in keeping with what is correct or proper

- **jubilant** (adj) joyful and proud especially because of triumph or success; full of high-spirited delight

- **maudlin** (adj) effusively or insincerely emotional

- **nuance** (n) a subtle difference in meaning or opinion or attitude

- **panacea** (n) hypothetical remedy for all ills or diseases

- **portent** (n) a sign of something about to happen

# Lesson 53                                                    Unit 9

Finish learning your vocabulary unit. Read each word and its definition. Use the space below each word to write a synonym, write a sentence containing the word, draw a picture, or use some other device to help you commit the definitions to memory.  You will have a quiz in Lesson 55.

- **prudent** (adj) careful and sensible; marked by sound judgment

- **reflect** (v) manifest or bring back; show an image of; give evidence of the quality of

- **serendipity** (n) good luck in making unexpected and fortunate discoveries

- **surmise** (n) a message expressing an opinion based on incomplete evidence; (v) infer from incomplete evidence; imagine to be the case

- **ubiquitous** (adj) being present everywhere at once

- **viscous** (adj) having a relatively high resistance to flow; having the sticky properties of an adhesive

Unscramble your vocabulary words. Study for your vocabulary quiz tomorrow. Make sure you know your words. Study ideas: read them out loud, copy the ones you are unsure of, have someone quiz you, use the words in conversation.

**Y I V A L N O T R A C**          _____
perceiving things beyond the natural range of the senses

**T I I N L B C M A O E P**          _____
not easy to combine harmoniously

**C A T V E A O D**          _____
a person who pleads for a cause

**T N C R O E T I**          _____
feeling or expressing pain or sorrow for sins or offenses

**P T N T E O R**          _____
a sign of something about to happen

**T E N M E I N**          _____
standing above others in quality or position

**D A M I U N L**          _____
effusively or insincerely emotional

**O I R G S R U G E A**          _____
instinctively seeking and enjoying the company of others

**I D U S U S O A S**          _____
marked by care and persistent effort

(continued on the next page)

ACEPANA
hypothetical remedy for all ills or diseases

_____

TENXEIUNGAT
lessen or try to lessen the seriousness or extent of

_____

UENCAN
a subtle difference in meaning or opinion or attitude

_____

TBLNUAJI
joyful and proud, especially because of triumph or success

_____

USPAHDAINO
so thin as to transmit light

_____

ERUTPND
careful and sensible

_____

SMUIERS
infer from incomplete evidence

_____

ESTDYIIENRP
good luck in making unexpected and fortunate discoveries

_____

RCLTEEF
manifest or bring back

_____

TQIUOUUSIB
being present everywhere at once

_____

UCSVIOS
having a relatively high resistance to flow

_____

# Lesson 55

You can study your words before you take this quiz, but you MUST put them away before you take the quiz. Cheaters get ZERO points for their quiz. Check your answers and record your score on your grade sheet.

Circle the letter that contains the word that *best* fits.

1. He was _____ in pointing out every detail.

    a. assiduous      b. diaphanous      c. gregarious      d. maudlin

2. She found it _____ to consult a financial advisor before investing.

    a. panacea      b. incompatible      c. prudent      d. clairvoyant

3. Cowboy hats are _____ in the country music scene.

    a. gregarious      b. viscous      c. ubiquitous      d. contrite

4. Cod liver oils is the time-honored _____.

    a. portent      b. panacea      c. surmise      d. nuance

5. A synonym for see-through.

    a. diaphanous      b. contrite      c. eminent      d. viscous

Fill in the blank with the word that *best* fits.

6. A subtle difference in meaning is known as _____.

7. To infer from incomplete evidence is to _____.

8. Being careful and sensible is being _____.

9. To be joyful and proud is to be _____.

10. Something having a relatively high resistance to flow is _____.

# Lesson 56                                          Units 7-9 Review

Look over all of your words and notes from the past three vocabulary units (7-9). Go over any rough spots in your memory.

# Lesson 57                                          Units 7-9 Review

Find a partner to help you with this review game. See if you can guess the vocabulary word in ten guesses or less. Guess letters one at a time for each word and have your partner fill them in or let you know they're not in the word.

— — — — — — — — —                    — — — — —
Hint: a disparaging remark                          Hint: subtle difference

— — — — — —                          — — — — — — —
Hint: dim or feeble                                 Hint: difficult to describe

— — — — — — — — —                    — — — — — —
Hint: marked by care                                Hint: not extinct

— — — — — — — —                      — — — — — —
Hint: expressing sorrow for sins                    Hint: a vague idea

— — — — — — — —                      — — — — — —
Hint: push for something                            Hint: declare as true

# Lesson 58                                                            Units 7-9 Review

Match the word to its definition.

1. adumbrate       _____ partially excusing or justifying

2. inveterate      _____ a corrupt act

3. extenuating     _____ surround so as to force to give up

4. ubiquitous      _____ of or involving dispute or controversy

5. turpitude       _____ describe roughly or briefly

6. devoid          _____ having a relatively high resistance to flow

7. desiccate       _____ someone who attacks in search of booty

8. scrutinize      _____ expressing offensive reproach

9. circumvent      _____ look at critically or searchingly

10. gregarious     _____ ostentatiously lofty in style

11. marauder       _____ so thin as to transmit light

12. egregious      _____ being present everywhere at once

13. polemic        _____ outrageously bad

14. diaphanous     _____ habitual

15. viscous        _____ completely wanting or lacking

16. scurrilous     _____ instinctively seeking and enjoying the company of others

17. turgid         _____ lacking vitality or spirit

# Lesson 59

Units 7-9 Review

Can you find all 60 of your vocabulary words in this massive word search? Flip back through the three units for the word list if you need it.

```
G Z G Q A G R A N D E U R Y V I N D I C T I V E K L L Y K T
J O A S P E R S I O N J D E R H H P Z S E I M P U T E V E T
P O R T E N T Q Y A S S I D U O U S Q Y C N M A N I F O L D
H A O D C T H F G T U R P I T U D E S A I U U N G S L T Z K
A M K T E B C L L V D E G R E G I O U S D N R A Q M A S D C
S A X J I S Q K N G Y M A U D L I N U D O V V R N B U N E C
S R W W U K I E Y D S E R E N D I P I T Y U O E I C Z V V Y
E A R S T B Z C M N I O A Q U Q E D C I D S F C C L E G O C
R U Z E D V I A C I I A U W E W X N C L A P Y C A T O D I O
T D P I D J C L V A N N P P F P T O E S A D X U I T I U D N
I E W U N U R I A M T E V H L B E T P X U I V I Z Y E V S T
K R R T P C N E R N N E N E A Q M I D O T P R E V L X L E I
Y I S H A A H D D C T R E T T N P O O W L E E V R O L B Q N
R L N C G B L O A E U S S D X E O N J G G E N R O S P W Q G
P Y P C R R V L A N E M V O I Q R U T C E J M U F Y I F R E
A R G R O U A J I T T M V L N S A A S D T J C I A L A T C N
Z D O Q O M T N Y D E Q G E Q G N G T K U E I X C T U N Y T
O E E X F V P I D T W Y S V N V E A U E R C R K Y O I O T B
D L G A I V O A N I S D L C M T O G R C G S C R W Z F N U C
C U P R P M C C T I L S E Q U W U M K L I U U E G O E J G S
O S L S E A I N A I Z O U W K B S T I D D R I F Y N Z D I F
N I E Y U G N T A T B E Q H D F I O R F L M T L N C D O O E
T V T J S R A A Y R I L K U E U S Q C L G I O E X M W J A X
R E H N K P F R C A U V E P E Y Y W U K H S U C S F D T Z T
I I O Q V O H E I E B M E V V N H Z M I E E S T H C E Q N A
T S R L Y K R C I O A Q O W M V C C O N T R A D I C T I O N
E H A S U A J I C T U I Q T X B A E R T X O I H L K D Z V T
O W R H Z Z Q N G F A S Z L P R U D E N T I U P P T F N I J
D R R V I S C O U S D B V I N D I C A T E U H S C U V F C O
P O A D U M B R A T E T X N N O W P V O P A L L I A T E E P
```

# Lesson 60                    Units 7-9 Review Quiz

If you got 100% on all three of your vocabulary quizzes so far, no vocab for you today. Way to go! If you didn't, take this review quiz. If you score higher on this than you did on one of your previous quizzes, you may replace the grade of one of those quizzes on your grade sheet (just one).

Circle the letter that contains the word that *best* fits.

1.  Will the Florida _____ be joining the assembly?

    a. grandeur      b. invective      c. contingent      d. surfeit

2.  The _____ display got us all in the Christmas spirit.

    a. jubilant      b. clairvoyant      c. redundant      d. circuitous

3.  The aspirin served to _____ his pain.

    a. impute      b. palliate      c. surfeit      d. reflect

4. The drama queen behaved in a _____ way toward even the smallest incident.

    a. prudent      b. incompatible      c. maudlin      d. inchoate

5.  The newspaper's _____ of the rally infuriated its organizers.

    a. invective      b. contingent      c. grandiloquence      d. panacea

Fill in the blank with the word that *best* fits.

6.  Extreme excess: _____.


7.  Something serving to provoke or excite is known as _____.


8.  Something that serves no useful purpose is _____.


9.  Something imperfectly formed is _____.


10.  A sign of something about to happen is a(n) _____.

# Lesson 61                                    Unit 10

Here is your next vocabulary unit. Read each word and its definition. Use the space below each word to write a synonym, write a sentence containing the word, draw a picture, or use some other device to help you commit the definitions to memory. You will have a quiz in Lesson 65.

- **aesthetic** (adj) characterized by an appreciation of beauty

- **assimilate** (v) become similar to one's environment; take up mentally

- **coalesce** (v) mix together different elements; fuse or cause to grow together

- **conundrum** (n) a difficult problem

- **differential** (n) a quality that differentiates between similar things; (adj) relating to or showing a difference; involving or containing one or more derivatives

- **empathy** (n) understanding and entering into another's feelings

- **extol** (v) praise, glorify, or honor

Continue learning your vocabulary unit. Read each word and its definition. Use the space below each word to write a synonym, write a sentence containing the word, draw a picture, or use some other device to help you commit the definitions to memory. You will have a quiz in Lesson 65.

- **hackneyed** (adj) repeated too often; overfamiliar through overuse

- **incongruous** (adj) lacking in harmony or compatibility or appropriateness

- **jubilation** (n) a feeling of extreme joy; a joyful occasion for special festivities to mark some happy event; the utterance of sounds expressing great joy

- **mawkish** (adj) insincerely emotional; maudlin

- **obdurate** (adj) stubbornly persistent in wrongdoing; showing unfeeling resistance to tender feelings

- **paragon** (n) an ideal instance; a perfect embodiment of a concept; one having no equal

- **pragmatic** (n) an imperial decree that becomes part of the fundamental law of the land; (adj) concerned with practical matters; guided by practical experience and observation rather than theory

# Lesson 63 Unit 10

Finish learning your vocabulary unit. Read each word and its definition. Use the space below each word to write a synonym, write a sentence containing the word, draw a picture, or use some other device to help you commit the definitions to memory. You will have a quiz in Lesson 65.

- **prurient** (adj) characterized by lust

- **rejuvenate** (v) make younger or more youthful; given new life or energy

- **servile** (adj) submissive or fawning in attitude or behavior; relating to or involving slaves

- **surreptitious** (adj) marked by quiet, caution, and secrecy; conducted with or marked by hidden aims or methods

- **umbrage** (n) a feeling of anger caused by being offended

- **vital** (adj) urgently needed; absolutely necessary; full of spirit; characteristic of life

# Lesson 64

Fill in the crossword puzzle with your vocabulary words. Study for your vocabulary quiz tomorrow. Make sure you know your words. Study ideas: read them out loud, copy the ones you are unsure of, have someone quiz you, use the words in conversation.

**Across:**
1. understanding another's feelings
4. submissive in attitude or behavior
6. a feeling of anger caused by being offended
8. a difficult problem
9. repeated too often
11. urgently needed
12. an ideal instance
14. lacking in harmony
16. insincerely emotional
17. concerned with practical matters
18. praise, glorify, or honor
19. make younger or more youthful
20. marked by hidden aims or methods

**Down:**
2. characterized by an appreciation of beauty
3. relating to or showing a difference
5. a feeling of extreme joy
7. characterized by lust
10. fuse or cause to grow together
13. become similar to one's environment
15. stubbornly persistent in wrongdoing

# Lesson 65                                      Unit 10 Quiz

You can study your words before you take this quiz, but you MUST put them away before you take the quiz. Cheaters get ZERO points for their quiz. Check your answers and record your score on your grade sheet.

Circle the letter that contains the word that *best* fits.

1.  I can't _____ to these cold winters!

      a. extol      b. rejuvenate      c.  aesthetic      d. assimilate

2.  Water and oil don't _____.

      a. coalesce      b. obdurate      c. servile      d. prurient

3.  The chef at Café Du Monde is a(n) _____.

      a. conundrum      b. paragon      c. jubilation      d. umbrage

4. Our dog has _____ ways of sneaking table scraps.

      a. surreptitious      b. vital      c. incongruous      d. pragmatic

5.  The weekend away will _____ your mind and body.

      a. extol      b. coalesce      c. rejuvenate      d. assimilate

Fill in the blank with the word that *best* fits.

6.  Something repeated too often is _____.

7.  A synonym for *maudlin* might be _____.

8.  A difficult problem is a(n) _____.

9.  A feeling of anger caused by being offended is known as _____.

10.  Something that's urgently needed is _____.

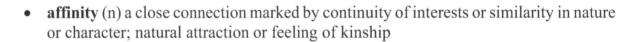

Here is your next vocabulary unit. Read each word and its definition. Use the space below each word to write a synonym, write a sentence containing the word, draw a picture, or use some other device to help you commit the definitions to memory.  You will have a quiz in Lesson 70.

- **affinity** (n) a close connection marked by continuity of interests or similarity in nature or character; natural attraction or feeling of kinship

- **asylum** (n) a shelter from danger or hardship; a hospital for the mentally incompetent

- **coalition** (n) the union of diverse things into one body or form or group; the state of being combined into one body

- **convergence** (n) the occurrence of two or more things coming together

- **differentiate** (v) mark as different; be a distinctive feature, attribute, or trait

- **empirical** (adj) derived from experiment and observation rather than theory; relying on medical quackery

- **fabricate** (v) put together out of artificial or natural components or parts; concoct something artificial or untrue

Continue learning your vocabulary unit. Read each word and its definition. Use the space below each word to write a synonym, write a sentence containing the word, draw a picture, or use some other device to help you commit the definitions to memory. You will have a quiz in Lesson 70.

- **hapless** (adj) deserving or inciting pity

- **inconsequential** (adj) lacking worth or importance; not following logically as a consequence

- **jumbled** (v) be all mixed up together; assembled without order or sense; (adj) in utter disorder

- **mendacious** (adj) given to lying; intentionally untrue

- **obfuscate** (v) make obscure or unclear

- **paramount** (adj) having superior power and influence

- **precarious** (adj) affording no ease or reassurance; fraught with danger; not secure

Finish learning your vocabulary unit. Read each word and its definition. Use the space below each word to write a synonym, write a sentence containing the word, draw a picture, or use some other device to help you commit the definitions to memory.  You will have a quiz in Lesson 70.

- **puerile** (adj) of or characteristic of a child; displaying or suggesting a lack of maturity

- **relegate** (v) refer to another person for decision or judgment; assign to a lower position

- **skeptical** (adj) denying or questioning something; marked by or given to doubt

- **sustainable** (adj) capable of being maintained at a certain rate or level

- **uniform** (n) clothing of distinctive design worn by a group; (adj) always the same; evenly spaced

- **vitriolic** (adj) harsh or corrosive in tone; capable of destroying or eating away by chemical action

# Lesson 69

Find your vocabulary words in the word search. As you find each one, repeat its definition. Look it up if you can't remember it. Study for your vocabulary quiz tomorrow. Make sure you know your words. Study ideas: read them out loud, copy the ones you are unsure of, have someone quiz you, use the words in conversation.

```
G B J X H Q A D R O T P O D O F T C Z K X P Q V D B U
X Y V H C V H R P S C H R M L B F C T T X V N Y C Y H
I B I A K H A V M I L M M P Y R F Q K U F T L S E E D
T J F P R F L P L Y B A T B G C G U M C S W I F F F I
I D Y L O H J O W M B B I H X U B P S J I R J C A M T
M I L E S X I U E Y S J A T D D U F G C Q H O U B P M
P P M S T R M N M U L E Y N N E P B S Q A T U G R B I
C Z X S T D D M S B C R E V R E J C V U K T I A I N F
X B C I W A E T I I L G L I J P U S F L R W E B C O W
V A V U C F A K K W J E L X G D M Q K U E C G Q A I B
I Q K I Q I C G U Y C E D E W P L O E O M L C I T T J
J Q O Q N R R O D N Q S S S O D Q A Z S M E A D E I A
L U M A N U X K N O E T A G E L E R C U N B B T V L P
S Y B U E T R K A V A J G A I E A F L I W O L U P A W
Q L N F M H J G C C E P T Y E O Y Y Y I T K C P S O N
E G M Q P G J J F D Y R U V L I S U A F E P I N C C X
R L N Y I X I J W P U K G Q B A T T E X O G E S I T P
N F X Z R G S U O I R A C E R P A Z U W R Q O K J F U
W X C E I X T A P Z H X B P N H L D T M P F N L S I I
V P U A C Y T I N I F F A W K C L U A Y H Z B O T M F
P O I Q A L G P A R A M O U N T E V H V E B T O H P R
R L G I L V Y T M R W U G A U W F J X B S N W F B W X
T B G L A U N I F O R M E P L E R I S Q M Y J Z H M O
B Q Y R I W K L P T Q W O S H I N G L H I T D U I V R
H W C C D R U N H N A T P Z F T Y B K N E B H Q N N R
Z L T I P C P J M Y M D J E A Q I L S D X O F O K C I
C A M F E D I F F E R E N T I A T E N G Y Y B D M N H
```

| | | | |
|---|---|---|---|
| affinity | empirical | mendacious | relegate |
| asylum | fabricate | obfuscate | skeptical |
| coalition | hapless | paramount | sustainable |
| convergence | inconsequential | precarious | uniform |
| differentiate | jumbled | puerile | vitriolic |

You can study your words before you take this quiz, but you MUST put them away before you take the quiz. Cheaters get ZERO points for their quiz. Check your answers and record your score on your grade sheet.

Circle the letter that contains the word that *best* fits.

1.  Don't _____ a story, just tell me what happened to the lamp.

    a. differentiate    b. obfuscate    c. relegate    d. fabricate

2.  The _____ of Jupiter and Saturn in the night sky was a sight to see.

    a. convergence    b. asylum    c. uniform    d. affinity

3.  The _____ passengers were stranded at the airport during the winter storm.

    a. empirical    b. mendacious    c. hapless    d. paramount

4. My words become _____ when I get nervous.

    a. precarious    b. jumbled    c. vitriolic    d. sustainable

5.  The _____ attack on the president was uncalled for.

    a. skeptical    b. vitriolic    c. empirical    d. precarious

Fill in the blank with the word that *best* fits.

6.  A shelter from danger or hardship is _____.

7.  To be given to lying is to be _____.

8.  When you make obscure or unclear, you _____.

9.  Displaying or suggesting a lack of maturity is _____.

10.  Having superior power or influence is being _____.

# Lesson 71                                                     Unit 12

Here is your next vocabulary unit. Read each word and its definition. Use the space below each word to write a synonym, write a sentence containing the word, draw a picture, or use some other device to help you commit the definitions to memory.  You will have a quiz in Lesson 75.

- **alacrity** (n) liveliness and eagerness

- **augment** (v) enlarge or increase; grow or intensify

- **cogent** (adj) powerfully persuasive

- **correlate** (n) either of two or more related or complementary variables; (v) to bear a reciprocal or mutual relation; (adj) mutually related

- **diffident** (adj) showing modest reserve; lacking self-confidence

- **enervate** (v) weaken mentally or morally; disturb the composure of

- **facetious** (adj) cleverly amusing in tone

Continue learning your vocabulary unit. Read each word and its definition. Use the space below each word to write a synonym, write a sentence containing the word, draw a picture, or use some other device to help you commit the definitions to memory. You will have a quiz in Lesson 75.

- **harangue** (n) a loud, bombastic declamation expressed with strong emotion; (v) address forcefully

- **incontrovertible** (adj) impossible to deny; necessarily or demonstrably true

- **jurisdiction** (n) law; in law, the territory within which power can be exercised

- **mercurial** (adj) liable to sudden unpredictable change; relating to or containing or caused by mercury

- **oblique** (n) a diagonally arranged abdominal muscle on either side of the torso; (adj) slanting; indirect in departing from the accepted or proper way; misleading

- **parched** (v) cause to wither or parch from exposure to heat; (adj) dried out by heat or excessive exposure to sunlight; extremely thirsty

- **precipitous** (adj) done with very great haste and without due deliberation; extremely steep

# Lesson 73          Unit 12

Finish learning your vocabulary unit. Read each word and its definition. Use the space below each word to write a synonym, write a sentence containing the word, draw a picture, or use some other device to help you commit the definitions to memory. You will have a quiz in Lesson 75.

- **pugnacious** (adj) tough and callous by virtue of experience; ready and able to resort to force or violence

- **relevant** (adj) having a bearing on or connection with the subject at issue

- **solicitous** (adj) full of anxiety and concern

- **sycophant** (n) a person who tries to please someone in order to gain a personal advantage

- **unilateral** (adj) involving only one part or side

- **vituperate** (v) spread negative information about

# Lesson 74

Unscramble your vocabulary words. Study for your vocabulary quiz tomorrow. Make sure you know your words. Study ideas: read them out loud, copy the ones you are unsure of, have someone quiz you, use the words in conversation.

R T E A U P V T E I

spread negative information about

_____

T R L E C O A E R

mutually related

_____

P O Y A H C S T N

a person who tries to please in order to gain personal advantage

_____

S I E P O R T C P U I

extremely steep

_____

O V I I B R L R E C T N E T N O

impossible to deny

_____

C A R A T L Y I

liveliness and eagerness

_____

B O E L U I Q

slanting

_____

T U S F C A I O E

cleverly amusing in tone

_____

O S I C U I O L S T

full of anxiety and concern

_____

(continued on the next page)

D E P C A R H

extremely thirsty

_____

E M N G T A U

enlarge or increase

_____

I U S N P G C O U A

tough by virtue of experience

_____

I T I F D E N D F

showing modest reserve

_____

G N R U H A E A

address forcefully

_____

O E T N G C

powerfully persuasive

_____

V N R E E A T E

weaken mentally or morally

_____

R C R A M L E U I

liable to sudden, unpredictable change

_____

O T R D S I J C I I U N

the territory within which power can be exercised

_____

T L I N U E A A L R

involving only one part or side

_____

T E L R A N E V

having a bearing on or connection with the subject at issue

# Lesson 75                                              Unit 12 Quiz

You can study your words before you take this quiz, but you MUST put them away before you take the quiz. Cheaters get ZERO points for their quiz. Check your answers and record your score on your grade sheet.

Circle the letter that contains the word that *best* fits.

1.  The _____ climb up the mountain left us all exhausted and thirsty.

     a. relevant       b. incontrovertible       c.  precipitous       d. facetious

2.  The doctor's _____ statement convinced me to get the surgery.

     a. diffident          b. cogent       c. mercurial       d. unilateral

3.  After a day of yard work in the sun, he was _____.

     a. parched       b. oblique       c. facetious       d. relevant

4. You can _____ your learning with various online options.

     a. harangue       b. vituperate       c. augment       d. correlate

5.  A synonym for *misleading*.

     a. pugnacious       b. oblique       c. mercurial       d. solicitous

Fill in the blank with the word that *best* fits.

6.  To be lacking self-confidence is to be _____.

7.  To address forcefully is to _____.

8.  A person who tries to please someone for personal gain is a(n) _____.

9.  Liveliness and eagerness is _____.

10.  Something involving only one part or side is _____.

# Lesson 76                                         Units 10-12 Review

Look over all of your words and notes from the past three vocabulary units (10-12). Go over any rough spots in your memory.

# Lesson 77                                         Units 10-12 Review

Find a partner to help you with this review game. See if you can guess the vocabulary word in ten guesses or less. Guess letters one at a time for each word and have your partner fill them in or let you know they're not in the word.

— — — — — — — — — — — —            — — — — — — —
Hint: make unclear                              Hint: powerfully persuasive


— — — — — — — — —                     — — — — — — — —
Hint: a shelter from danger                     Hint: insincerely emotional


— — — — — — — — — — — —            — — — — — —
Hint: liable to sudden, unpredictable change         Hint: full of spirit


— — — — — — — — — —                   — — — — — —
Hint: cause to grow together                     Hint: praise, glorify


— — — — — — — — — —                   — — — — — — —
Hint: natural attraction                         Hint: inciting pity

# Lesson 78

Match the word to its definition.

1. obdurate     \_\_\_\_\_ liveliness and eagerness

2. empirical     \_\_\_\_\_ a feeling of anger caused by being offended

3. alacrity     \_\_\_\_\_ marked by quiet, caution, and secrecy

4. vituperate     \_\_\_\_\_ derived from experiment or observation rather than theory

5. puerile     \_\_\_\_\_ a difficult problem

6. servile     \_\_\_\_\_ harsh or corrosive in tone

7. umbrage     \_\_\_\_\_ given to lying

8. precarious     \_\_\_\_\_ displaying a lack of maturity

9. vitriolic     \_\_\_\_\_ weaken mentally or morally

10. oblique     \_\_\_\_\_ stubbornly persistent in wrongdoing

11. convergence     \_\_\_\_\_ repeated too often

12. surreptitious     \_\_\_\_\_ submissive in attitude or behavior

13. mendacious     \_\_\_\_\_ misleading

14. conundrum     \_\_\_\_\_ spread negative information about

15. hackneyed     \_\_\_\_\_ address forcefully

16. enervate     \_\_\_\_\_ the occurrence of two or more things coming together

17. harangue     \_\_\_\_\_ fraught with danger

# Lesson 79

Can you find all 60 of your vocabulary words in this massive word search? Flip back through the three units for the word list if you need it.

```
B C J S V Y I L U M V P C O R R E L A T E G I N P F S D H K
O T O I K H P X E V S O L I C I T O U S N T A U Q U H G A J
O W T Z N E I N C O N S E Q U E N T I A L V X N M Y X K P H
F E A W Y C P W T R M M R Q L V L P R E C I P I T O U S L S
I N F L H O O T T C H A M S R T F S F X I A Z F D T Y W E E
N E F H P N Q N I F Q A O S M L L X F T G W U O I U A W S R
C R I A A U P S T C N D K F A B R I C A T E K R F L U B S V
O V N C R N R Y J R A P P H A R A N G U E D Z M F H G C K I
N A I K A D E C K M O L B I R F W E L K L X B Q E R M E D L
G T T N M R C O O T Q V M E N D A C I O U S V H R D E N W E
R E Y E O U A P A S P Z E Z Y Y J W W Q D X Q F E O N H L A
U K X Y U M R H A S L J O R B M R E L E V A N T N B T C V V
O C M E N B I A J U B I L A T I O N I A S Q U G T L A O U L
U M H D T V O N O R A X J U R I S D I C T I O N I I L N N S
S F R I Z X U T S R O E H J E Z B V W G N Z U X A Q A V I U
E D E F E M S D J E C A B U X O W L M E X H O D T U C E L S
M F J F I P V K Q P M S P M T B C D E S M Z Y Y E R R A T
P A U I P A I C C T J S U B O D T E M P I R I C A L I G T A
A C V D D R T R M I A I E L L U V I T U P E R A T E T E E I
T E E E I C A G P T E M R E H R O B F U S C A T E T Y N R N
H T N N F H L P R I S I I D R A V I T R I O L I C P V C A A
Y I A T F E B A U O T L L O E T G E H E G L N H V C P E L B
F O T S E D C R R U H A E D L E P F F U M W I K U O R Y N L
M U E N R T O A I S E T H Q E B D I C T S P L K M A A I K E
G S B X E A G G E H T E P U G N A C I O U S C Z B L G Z M E
A D G V N S E O N J I R G O A M E R C U R I A L R I M D H W
C W J V T Y N N T H C D J V T M A W K I S H K J A T A P Z F
P M B P I L T V N L E N Q Q E S P R I N U Z X D G I T V O K
A W G S A U C O A L E S C E T T J K Q G S V A O E O I C B G
B K G E L M T T I C Q J F B P R K S T Z I F D T C N C O X K
```

# Lesson 80                Units 10-12 Review Quiz

If you got 100% on all three of your vocabulary quizzes so far, no vocab for you today. Way to go! If you didn't, take this review quiz. If you score higher on this than you did on one of your previous quizzes, you may replace the grade of one of those quizzes on your grade sheet (just one).

Circle the letter that contains the word that *best* fits.

1.  The scientist had a _____ approach to dealing with the water shortage.

    a. pragmatic      b. prurient      c. facetious      d. correlate

2.  The _____ inquiry about my health was appreciated.

    a. unilateral      b. skeptical      c. solicitous      d. incongruous

3.  The _____ of business owners sponsored a scholarship.

    a. differential      b. coalition      c. jurisdiction      d. sycophant

4. Playing in the basketball game left me _____.

    a. parched      b. precipitous      c. relevant      d. incongruous

5.  The _____ mess of a room took hours to clean.

    a. pugnacious      b. incontrovertible      c. sustainable      d. jumbled

Fill in the blank with the word that *best* fits.

6.  A synonym for law could be _____.

7.  Something that's capable of being maintained at a certain level is _____.

8.  To give new life or energy is to _____.

9.  To become similar to one's environment is to _____.

10.  A perfect embodiment of a concept is a(n) _____.

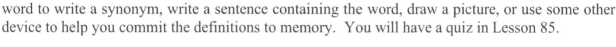

Here is your next vocabulary unit. Read each word and its definition. Use the space below each word to write a synonym, write a sentence containing the word, draw a picture, or use some other device to help you commit the definitions to memory. You will have a quiz in Lesson 85.

- **aloof** (adj) remote in manner; (adv) in a distant or remote manner

- **authentic** (adj) conforming to fact and therefore worthy of belief; not counterfeit or copied; real

- **cohesive** (adj) well-integrated; sticking or holding together and resisting separation

- **credulity** (n) tendency to believe readily

- **diffuse** (v) move outward; cause to become widely known; (adj) spread out; not concentrated in one place; lacking conciseness

- **enhance** (v) increase; make better or more attractive

- **facilitate** (v) make easier; be of use; increase the likelihood of

Continue learning your vocabulary unit. Read each word and its definition. Use the space below each word to write a synonym, write a sentence containing the word, draw a picture, or use some other device to help you commit the definitions to memory.  You will have a quiz in Lesson 85.

- **hardship** (n) a state of affliction; something hard to endure; something that causes or entails suffering

- **indefatigable** (adj) showing sustained enthusiastic action with unflagging vitality

- **jury** (n) a body of citizens sworn to give a true verdict according to the evidence presented in a court of law; a committee appointed to judge a competition

- **meticulous** (adj) marked by precise accordance with details

- **oblivious** (adj) failing to keep in mind

- **pariah** (n) a person who is rejected from society or home

- **preclude** (v) keep from happening or arising; make impossible, especially beforehand

# Lesson 83 Unit 13

Finish learning your vocabulary unit. Read each word and its definition. Use the space below each word to write a synonym, write a sentence containing the word, draw a picture, or use some other device to help you commit the definitions to memory. You will have a quiz in Lesson 85.

- **pulchritude** (n) physical beauty (especially of women)

- **relinquish** (v) part with a possession or right; do without or cease to adhere to; turn away from; release

- **solidarity** (n) a union of interests or purposes or sympathies among members of a group

- **tacit** (adj) implied or inferred from actions or statements

- **uninspired** (adj) having no intellectual, emotional, or spiritual excitement; deficient in originality or creativity; lacking powers of invention

- **void** (n) the state of nonexistence; an empty area or space; (v) declare invalid; (adj) lacking any legal or binding force; containing nothing

# Lesson 84

# Unit 13 Practice

Fill in the crossword puzzle with your vocabulary words. Study for your vocabulary quiz tomorrow. Make sure you know your words. Study ideas: read them out loud, copy the ones you are unsure of, have someone quiz you, use the words in conversation.

**Across:**
2. a person who is rejected from society
4. cause to become widely known
8. marked by precise accordance with details
10. remote in manner
11. make better or more attractive
12. an empty area or space
16. tendency to believe readily
18. real
19. keep from happening or arising

**Down**:
1. sticking or holding together
3. a state of affliction
5. increase the likelihood of
6. deficient in originality or creativity
7. union of interests of group members
9. failing to keep in mind
13. physical beauty, especially of women
14. a group chosen to judge a competition
15. implied or inferred from actions or statements
17. part with a possession or right

# Lesson 85

You can study your words before you take this quiz, but you MUST put them away before you take the quiz. Cheaters get ZERO points for their quiz. Check your answers and record your score on your grade sheet.

Circle the letter that contains the word that *best* fits.

1.  The new ramp will _____ the entry of wheelchairs into the building.

    a. diffuse     b. preclude     c. facilitate     d. relinquish

2.  The beautiful flowers were at the height of their _____.

    a. pariah     b. pulchritude     c. void     d. credulity

3. A synonym for *increase*.

    a. enhance     b. diffuse     c. preclude     d. relinquish

4. Her _____ planning saved the day when the rain threatened to ruin the party.

    a. oblivious     b. aloof     c. meticulous     d. authentic

5. The injury will _____ him from an athletic career.

    a. preclude     b. diffuse     c. enhance     d. facilitate

Fill in the blank with the word that *best* fits.

6. Remote in manner is _____.

7. Sticking or holding together and resisting separation is being _____.

8. A tendency to believe readily is _____.

9. A union of interests or purposes is known as _____.

10. A person who is rejected from society or home is a(n) _____.

Here is your next vocabulary unit. Read each word and its definition. Use the space below each word to write a synonym, write a sentence containing the word, draw a picture, or use some other device to help you commit the definitions to memory. You will have a quiz in Lesson 90.

- **alternative** (n) one of a number of things from which only one can be chosen; (adj) serving or used in place of another

- **befall** (v) become of; happen to

- **collaborate** (v) work together on a common project; cooperate

- **criterion** (n) a basis for comparison; a reference point against which other things can be evaluated; the ideal terms of which something can be judged

- **digression** (n) a message that departs from the main subject; a turning aside; wandering from the main path of a journey

- **ephemeral** (n) anything short-lived; (adj) lasting a very short time

- **fallacious** (adj) intended to deceive; based on an incorrect or misleading notion or information

# Lesson 87 Unit 14

Continue learning your vocabulary unit. Read each word and its definition. Use the space below each word to write a synonym, write a sentence containing the word, draw a picture, or use some other device to help you commit the definitions to memory. You will have a quiz in Lesson 90.

- **haughty** (adj) having or showing arrogant superiority to and disdain of those one views as unworthy

- **indigenous** (adj) originating where it is found

- **justify** (v) show to be right by providing proof; declare innocent; adjust the spaces between words

- **mishap** (n) an unpredictable outcome that is unfortunate

- **obscure** (v) make less visible or unclear; (adj) not clearly expressed or understood

- **parsimony** (n) extreme care in spending money; extreme stinginess

- **precocious** (adj) characterized by or characteristic of exceptionally early development or maturity, especially in mental aptitude

Finish learning your vocabulary unit. Read each word and its definition. Use the space below each word to write a synonym, write a sentence containing the word, draw a picture, or use some other device to help you commit the definitions to memory.  You will have a quiz in Lesson 90.

- **punctilious** (adj) marked by precise accordance with details

- **renovate** (v) restore to a previous or better condition; make brighter and prettier; give new life or energy to

- **solipsistic** (adj) believing that only the self exists

- **taciturn** (adj) habitually reserved and uncommunicative

- **unprecedented** (adj) never done or known before; novel

- **wanton** (n) lewd or lascivious woman; (v) waste time; spend wastefully; behave brutally; (adj) occurring without motivation or provocation

# Lesson 89

Find your vocabulary words in the word search. As you find each one, repeat its definition. Look it up if you can't remember it. Study for your vocabulary quiz tomorrow. Make sure you know your words. Study ideas: read them out loud, copy the ones you are unsure of, have someone quiz you, use the words in conversation.

```
L  S  T  K  F  N  M  U  Y  A  H  P  L  W  R  W  U  H  T  N  X  J  C  G  Q
D  F  E  O  F  V  C  M  A  M  X  I  J  O  G  B  P  W  W  O  E  I  S  I  S
I  A  N  G  Y  T  G  N  H  K  R  A  S  V  K  X  N  T  I  V  C  U  A  N  M
G  L  Y  R  B  O  B  S  C  U  R  E  F  W  V  K  E  G  I  B  O  D  Y  S  E
R  L  P  C  B  R  L  B  O  L  A  T  R  Q  P  N  X  T  L  N  L  X  X  D  P
E  A  D  V  X  E  E  Y  M  L  N  A  X  X  E  Z  A  C  E  P  L  L  U  T  H
S  C  B  U  P  V  B  U  I  R  I  S  U  O  S  N  B  G  W  X  A  K  C  P  E
S  I  E  U  J  D  P  Y  U  B  Z  P  Y  P  R  H  I  N  Z  E  B  D  R  D  M
I  O  F  K  G  R  U  T  D  Q  C  R  S  E  A  D  N  R  H  K  O  U  I  X  E
O  U  A  U  I  U  I  Y  O  K  P  S  T  I  N  R  K  T  J  K  R  Z  T  H  R
N  S  L  H  O  C  D  E  W  N  G  L  U  I  S  P  S  W  I  I  A  M  E  E  A
C  W  L  N  A  U  W  V  D  Z  A  T  J  K  K  T  P  I  A  Q  T  H  R  O  L
G  B  P  T  Q  O  J  G  H  Z  P  Z  X  N  O  V  I  S  M  N  E  S  I  R  P
N  R  R  L  F  B  A  H  N  K  R  P  T  S  R  V  J  C  O  O  T  J  O  E  J
N  Q  I  P  G  A  Q  I  I  J  E  M  C  D  A  D  Q  T  T  N  N  O  N  N  J
I  X  L  B  S  W  A  P  O  G  C  Z  P  V  K  E  U  P  P  U  S  Y  N  O  J
E  C  P  M  X  Q  K  F  R  S  O  R  V  X  M  L  U  U  M  M  A  H  P  V  C
M  Q  X  B  M  S  E  P  J  N  C  V  H  G  L  X  I  J  I  T  N  J  A  A  R
O  S  H  X  N  P  U  N  C  T  I  L  I  O  U  S  W  F  S  E  N  U  A  T  E
Y  W  G  B  Z  V  M  C  N  J  O  F  P  K  E  U  D  M  H  L  N  S  X  E  C
N  H  A  U  G  H  T  Y  T  N  U  B  H  Y  Z  W  N  J  A  I  R  T  P  M  V
M  E  R  A  W  Q  K  F  M  S  S  X  P  F  R  E  F  C  P  Y  F  I  J  M  R
X  D  D  C  X  U  L  I  R  S  W  G  H  Q  P  D  Q  J  C  H  U  F  M  J  D
U  K  C  O  R  T  F  I  U  N  P  R  E  C  E  D  E  N  T  E  D  Y  A  K  G
R  T  E  I  P  F  P  J  B  O  Z  Z  Q  V  G  Y  G  W  P  H  Y  A  G  T  P
```

| alternative | ephemeral | mishap | renovate |
| befall | fallacious | obscure | solipsistic |
| collaborate | haughty | parsimony | taciturn |
| criterion | indigenous | precocious | unprecedented |
| digression | justify | punctilious | wanton |

# Lesson 90

You can study your words before you take this quiz, but you MUST put them away before you take the quiz. Cheaters get ZERO points for their quiz. Check your answers and record your score on your grade sheet.

Circle the letter that contains the word that *best* fits.

1.  The _____ with my computer cost me 10 hours of work.

    a. alternative       b. criterion       c. wanton       d. mishap

2.  The _____ kindergartener won the K-5 spelling bee.

    a. obscure       b. precocious       c. fallacious       d. solipsistic

3.  The neighbors decided to _____ to relocate the pesky chipmunk.

    a. collaborate       b. befall       c. obscure       d. justify

4. We will _____ the kitchen to get it the way we want it.

    a. wanton       b. renovate       c. ephemeral       d. indigenous

5.  It was a giant _____ when we ended up discussing math in Spanish class.

    a. criterion       b. fallacious       c. digression       d. unprecedented

Fill in the blank with the word that *best* fits.

6.  Believing that only the self exists is _____.

7.  Marked by precise accordance with details is _____.

8.  Extreme stinginess is _____.

9.  Something lasting a very short time is _____.

10.  Something that has never been done or known before is _____.

# Lesson 91 Unit 15

Here is your next vocabulary unit. Read each word and its definition. Use the space below each word to write a synonym, write a sentence containing the word, draw a picture, or use some other device to help you commit the definitions to memory. You will have a quiz in Lesson 95.

- **ambiguous** (adj) open to interpretation; often intended to mislead; having more than one possible meaning

- **belligerent** (n) someone who fights; (adj) characteristic of one eager to fight

- **compassion** (n) a deep awareness of and sympathy for another's suffering

- **critical** (adj) marked by a tendency to find and call attention to errors and flaws; characterized by careful evaluation and judgment; urgently needed; being in a state of crisis or emergency

- **diligent** (adj) quietly and steadily persevering, especially in detail or exactness; characterized by care and perseverance in carrying out tasks

- **equitable** (adj) fair to all parties as dictated by reason or conscience

- **fastidious** (adj) giving careful attention to detail; hard to please; excessively concerned with cleanliness

Continue learning your vocabulary unit. Read each word and its definition. Use the space below each word to write a synonym, write a sentence containing the word, draw a picture, or use some other device to help you commit the definitions to memory. You will have a quiz in Lesson 95.

- **hedonist** (n) someone motivated by desires for sensual pleasures


- **indiscriminate** (adj) failing to make or recognize distinctions; not marked by fine distinctions


- **languor** (n) a relaxed, comfortable feeling; oppressively still air; a feeling of lack of interest or energy


- **modicum** (n) a small or moderate amount


- **obsequious** (adj) attempting to win favor from influential people by flattery


- **pathos** (n) a quality that arouses emotions, especially pity or sorrow; a feeling of sympathy or sorrow for the misfortunes of others; a style that has the power to evoke feelings


- **prescient** (adj) perceiving the significance of events before they occur

Finish learning your vocabulary unit. Read each word and its definition. Use the space below each word to write a synonym, write a sentence containing the word, draw a picture, or use some other device to help you commit the definitions to memory. You will have a quiz in Lesson 95.

- **pungent** (adj) strong and sharp; capable of wounding

- **reprobate** (n) a person without moral scruples; (v) express strong disapproval of; (adj) deviating from what is considered moral or right

- **solution** (n) a homogeneous mixture of two or more substances; a statement that solves a problem

- **tactful** (adj) having or showing a sense of what is fitting and considerate; showing skill and sensitivity in dealing with people

- **unrealized** (adj) marked by failure to realize full potentialities

- **wary** (adj) marked by keen caution and watchful prudence; openly distrustful and unwilling to confide

# Lesson 94

Unscramble your vocabulary words. Study for your vocabulary quiz tomorrow. Make sure you know your words. Study ideas: read them out loud, copy the ones you are unsure of, have someone quiz you, use the words in conversation.

**A Y R W**
marked by keen caution and watchful prudence

_____

**A T O S H P**
a quality that arouses emotions, especially pity or sorrow

_____

**R G N U L O A**
a relaxed, comfortable feeling

_____

**C U D M M O I**
a small or moderate amount

_____

**G E N P N T U**
strong and sharp

_____

**L A T U T F C**
having or showing a sense of what is fitting and considerate

_____

**R C T C I L I A**
marked by a tendency to find and call attention to errors and flaws

_____

**D N L E T I I G**
quietly and steadily persevering, especially in detail or exactness

_____

**I D S T O H E N**
someone motivated by desires for sensual pleasures

_____

(continued on the next page)

O L U S I O T N

a statement that solves a problem

_____

A B I O G U U S M

open to interpretation

_____

Q B L E I A U T E

fair to all parties as dictated by reason or conscience

_____

I P E R N T S C E

perceiving the significance of events before they occur

_____

T R E O E P A R B

 deviating from what is considered moral or right

_____

O M A N P C O S I S

a deep awareness of and sympathy for another's suffering

_____

S T U S O I A I D F

giving careful attention to detail

_____

Q S S I U O O U B E

attempting to win favor from influential people by flattery

_____

Z I A E U R L N E D

marked by failure to realize full potentialities

_____

B L N R E I E L E G T

someone who fights

_____

D S T A N I R M E I I I N C

failing to make or recognize distinctions

_____

# Lesson 95                                    Unit 15 Quiz

You can study your words before you take this quiz, but you MUST put them away before you take the quiz. Cheaters get ZERO points for their quiz. Check your answers and record your score on your grade sheet.

Circle the letter that contains the word that *best* fits.

1.  The _____ child was constantly in time out.
    a. ambiguous      b. belligerent      c. fastidious      d. obsequious

2.  The _____ nature of the instructions made them difficult to follow.
    a. pungent      b. prescient      c. ambiguous      d. wary

3.  We felt a _____ of relief with the test over, though the results were still to come.
    a. modicum      b. pathos      c. solution      d. hedonist

4.  My disorderly ways were quickly nipped in the bud by my _____ roommate.
    a. fastidious      b. equitable      c. reprobate      d. unrealized

5.  I fondly remember the _____ of sunny days at the lake.
    a. belligerent      b. compassion      c. modicum      d. languor

Fill in the blank with the word that *best* fits.

6.  A quality that arouses pity or sorrow is _____.

7.  Something deviating from what is considered moral or right is _____.

8.  To be marked by keen caution and watchful prudence is to be _____.

9.  To show sensitivity in dealing with people is to be _____.

10. A deep awareness of and sympathy for another's suffering is _____.

# Lesson 96         Units 13-15 Review

Look over all of your words and notes from the past three vocabulary units (13-15). Go over any rough spots in your memory.

# Lesson 97         Units 13-15 Review

Find a partner to help you with this review game. See if you can guess the vocabulary word in ten guesses or less. Guess letters one at a time for each word and have your partner fill them in or let you know they're not in the word.

\_\_ \_\_ \_\_ \_\_ \_\_ \_\_ \_\_ \_\_ \_\_ \_\_       \_\_ \_\_ \_\_ \_\_ \_\_ \_\_ \_\_

Hint: tendency to believe readily       Hint: happen to

\_\_ \_\_ \_\_ \_\_ \_\_ \_\_ \_\_       \_\_ \_\_ \_\_ \_\_ \_\_ \_\_ \_\_

Hint: a quality that arouses pity       Hint: strong and sharp

\_\_ \_\_ \_\_ \_\_ \_\_ \_\_ \_\_ \_\_       \_\_ \_\_ \_\_ \_\_ \_\_ \_\_

Hint: extreme stinginess       Hint: implied from actions

\_\_ \_\_ \_\_ \_\_ \_\_ \_\_ \_\_ \_\_       \_\_ \_\_ \_\_ \_\_ \_\_ \_\_ \_\_

Hint: well-integrated       Hint: unfortunate, unpredictable outcome

\_\_ \_\_ \_\_ \_\_ \_\_ \_\_ \_\_ \_\_ \_\_       \_\_ \_\_ \_\_ \_\_ \_\_ \_\_

Hint: someone motivated by sensual desires       Hint: spend wastefully

# Lesson 98

Match the word to its definition.

1. aloof         _____ showing a sense of what is fitting and considerate

2. digression    _____ increase

3. tactful       _____ lasting a very short time

4. languor      _____ a relaxed, comfortable feeling

5. reprobate     _____ a small or moderate amount

6. pungent      _____ physical beauty

7. enhance      _____ marked by precise accordance with details

8. obscure      _____ remote in manner

9. pulchritude   _____ characteristic of exceptionally early development

10. ephemeral    _____ make less visible or unclear

11. indiscriminate _____ open to interpretation

12. modicum     _____ a person without moral scruples

13. indigenous    _____ originating where it is found

14. meticulous    _____ perceiving the significance of events before they occur

15. precocious    _____ a message that departs from the main subject

16. ambiguous    _____ failing to make or recognize distinctions

17. prescient     _____ capable of wounding

# Lesson 99

Units 13-15 Review

Can you find all 60 of your vocabulary words in this massive word search? Flip back through the three units for the word list if you need it.

```
W Y O N H U J A D E F V C X Z J P I R E L I N Q U I S H R G
U S B O Y I L L Y I O Y Z U L J V U N N D H S X C C A E I N
G T L X B E O H A U G H T Y D Y S D N D S M P J E R X S H B
U W I L L S K B F K J R U O U A V P F C E P T T X G X O D A
F Y V W R P E C S A E Q E N U E M F R X T F U A V R V L I L
A B I S C B U Q R C L I R S P M P B C E R I A T Y V H U L O
C R O O R E V L U E U L M F S R X H I H C D L T G Q P T I O
I E U L I F N E C I D R A C U I E X E G E O A I I U L I G F
L P S I T A C K S H O U E C G X O C M M U N C D O G F O E C
I R K D I L T O K Y R U L L I B H N E M E O H I F U A N N R
T O R A C L A M L D E I S I H O T S T D O R U A O R S B T I
A B K R A P C V C L C Q T X T K U A I Q E D A S N U W W L T
T A A I L A I R O T A J Q U T Y F S C O E N I L C C S I R E
E T J T N T T F M A W B U T D P F V U I U V T C S G E J E R
A E V Y O H U R P C K A O S P E R O L J T X B E U B M F N I
E L S T T O R X A T Z N N R T G Y I O L S L I B D M B X O O
H I T O G S N K S F D O G T A I U D U P A R S I M O N Y V N
N I D E L G F P S U O Y Z F O T F N S N J Y L S Q C B K A C
E H N S R I S K I L S Y Y K E N E Y I F M I S H A P H Q T B
U Q H D K N P I O I N D I S C R I M I N A T E O Y N E B E S
X N U Q I P A S N W Q P J X H M L L A V S H G L W F D E Q U
T X R I Y G R T I Y U Z T V P I A W U Z Z P S A P A O L C C
N R H E T F E E I S V B L W R V N A T N M A I N Y S N L U O
H W U D A A N N C V T G U F E I G R H Q H R D R J T I I U H
E J H W D L B L O L E I D R S I U Y E K E I E H E I S G T E
M C P D R H I L Z U U E C V C F O U N U L A C L C D T E D S
P U N G E N T Z E H S D N J I T R Q T M G H V Y U I N R G I
L A D I F F U S E B W Y E U E C M F I T F X A P D O E E U V
P U R I K S Z O W D L C P R N A R I C V F J U H O U I N I E
X K Y Y H A R D S H I P C Y T M L I Q O F Q G B Z S A T T N
```

# Lesson 100                    Units 13-15 Review Quiz

If you got 100% on all three of your vocabulary quizzes so far, no vocab for you today. Way to go! If you didn't, take this review quiz. If you score higher on this than you did on one of your previous quizzes, you may replace the grade of one of those quizzes on your grade sheet (just one).

Circle the letter that contains the word that *best* fits.

1.  We were _____ to the trail of ants coming in overnight.

    a. uninspired       b. oblivious       c. haughty       d. obsequious

2.  The _____ didn't gel as much as the chemist had anticipated.

    a. solution       b. compassion       c. criterion       d. pariah

3.  Splitting all the candy was the most _____ thing I could think of.

    a. fastidious       b. fallacious       c. indefatigable       d. equitable

4.  The toddler didn't want to _____ his sister's toy.

    a. preclude       b. collaborate       c. relinquish       d. justify

5.  With _____ studying, he received a great score on the SAT.

    a. solipsistic       b. taciturn       c. diligent       d. uninspired

Fill in the blank with the word that *best* fits.

6.  Showing sustained enthusiastic action is being _____.

7.  To work together on a common project is to _____.

8.  Characteristic of one eager to fight: _____.

9.  Something intended to deceive is _____.

10.  To restore to a previous or better position is to _____.

Find a partner to help you with this review game. See if you can guess the vocabulary word in ten guesses or less. Guess letters one at a time for each word and have your partner fill them in or let you know they're not in the word.

— — — — — — — — —
Hint: worthy of imitation

— — — — — — —
Hint: turn aside

— — — — — — —
Hint: easily managed

— — — — — — —
Hint: demanding attention

— — — — — — — —
Hint: lasting a short time

— — — — — — — —
Hint: sour or bitter in taste

— — — — — — —
Hint: the way a person behaves

— — — — — — —
Hint: show in a picture

— — — — — — — —
Hint: existing only in the mind

— — — — — —
Hint: lacking wit

— — — — — — — —
Hint: something of little value

— — — — — —
Hint: a person who delivers a speech

# Lesson 102

Match the word to its definition.

1. paragon _____ insincerely emotional

2. servile _____ concoct something artificial or untrue

3. assimilate _____ liveliness and eagerness

4. extol _____ become similar to one's environment

5. mawkish _____ make obscure or unclear

6. surreptitious _____ submissive or fawning in attitude or behavior

7. fabricate _____ weaken mentally or morally

8. relegate _____ given to lying

9. obfuscate _____ extremely steep

10. mendacious _____ an ideal instance

11. precarious _____ liable to sudden unpredictable change

12. alacrity _____ address forcefully

13. mercurial _____ praise, glorify, or honor

14. enervate _____ assign to a lower position

15. sycophant _____ marked by quiet, caution, and secrecy

16. precipitous _____ fraught with danger

17. harangue _____ a person who tries to please someone for personal gain

# Lesson 103

Units 4-6 Review

Can you find the listed words from Units 4-6 in this word search? Say the definition as you circle the word. If you can't, go back and look it up before moving on.

```
S  D  K  H  O  M  V  I  C  I  S  S  I  T  U  D  E  A  H  W  U  A  V  L  Q  D  M  W  J
Y  H  D  T  P  N  A  R  Q  Y  M  N  J  T  O  P  H  H  N  T  J  W  C  S  Q  T  E  Y  S
H  I  P  Y  A  U  R  E  T  R  U  C  U  L  E  N  T  K  G  O  V  Q  E  P  I  K  E  R  U
S  E  R  U  I  D  K  T  L  J  J  X  P  D  D  V  E  E  G  T  N  J  F  V  V  V  X  B  C
D  T  O  B  B  K  H  I  H  S  V  J  E  B  T  Y  K  C  N  O  U  C  B  W  Z  L  S  C  C
I  N  T  T  A  T  A  M  X  P  T  J  X  H  U  U  S  E  S  P  R  D  H  F  Z  L  W  B  O
M  H  E  A  A  X  R  P  B  L  O  R  W  M  G  M  D  F  O  B  A  D  X  A  F  F  K  Q  R
G  Y  A  E  W  R  L  I  X  Q  N  P  O  M  P  U  J  K  Q  S  T  Y  F  V  L  E  X  N  Y
C  H  N  N  O  D  Z  H  L  O  O  E  B  M  P  D  E  S  W  E  X  L  R  Y  M  A  Q  J  Y
S  A  N  G  U  I  N  E  I  A  N  I  P  M  R  J  U  P  A  R  R  O  G  A  T  E  N  E  V
C  T  F  X  M  L  X  T  K  O  T  V  I  U  X  O  L  T  T  D  Q  Y  N  A  K  F  H  T  U
J  N  F  Q  B  I  C  M  S  J  T  E  B  T  I  T  A  C  U  M  E  N  J  N  Z  P  C  D  L
R  O  A  D  B  N  J  L  R  D  W  J  R  T  S  I  P  F  D  E  R  O  G  A  T  O  R  Y  J
U  P  W  P  A  G  R  W  Y  Q  E  T  A  A  I  B  A  U  M  A  L  L  E  A  B  L  E  I  W
I  I  Z  S  P  G  J  T  L  S  G  T  L  I  L  Z  V  E  X  P  I  A  T  E  C  U  X  P  H
E  W  A  N  R  R  Z  S  R  O  N  J  T  Z  Q  V  I  L  I  F  Y  T  M  O  W  D  Q  O  S
F  D  O  H  F  Z  O  E  O  E  O  P  S  A  N  C  T  I  M  O  N  I  O  U  S  H  B  J  A
F  K  N  Y  S  C  U  B  T  B  N  Y  W  I  B  S  N  R  M  X  O  R  F  K  N  A  B  Q  D
R  E  A  U  U  Y  S  A  Y  L  C  W  I  B  B  L  G  E  H  N  G  R  M  W  V  C  Z  U
O  I  I  W  K  U  O  W  N  T  S  L  H  Z  W  U  Q  L  O  J  R  F  S  Y  M  R  N  L  L
N  I  A  B  E  L  J  O  W  Z  I  M  J  A  L  F  B  N  I  U  C  G  N  C  I  G  W  A  A
T  O  K  T  Y  V  C  Y  L  L  I  O  T  Y  N  A  Q  J  C  W  O  I  H  L  M  Q  L  S  T
E  Y  E  G  O  C  E  N  T  R  I  C  N  Y  C  T  U  O  Q  A  C  F  G  L  P  L  E  C  I
R  T  W  Q  K  O  P  Y  K  G  L  G  W  A  D  C  Q  P  R  O  S  P  E  R  I  T  Y  E  O
Y  H  P  J  Q  D  N  Q  D  R  J  F  L  O  A  I  Q  F  M  C  G  R  H  P  N  G  K  T  N
I  S  K  S  U  D  B  N  S  M  A  P  A  M  W  U  Y  F  V  K  Z  E  Y  D  G  F  Z  I  S
I  Q  U  D  F  C  Y  Z  D  X  M  H  B  R  M  V  H  S  R  Q  D  E  T  X  E  O  D  C  I
V  I  C  A  R  I  O  U  S  I  X  J  G  T  R  D  E  P  R  E  C  A  T  E  G  D  Y  C  O
U  E  M  E  G  C  Z  U  J  V  U  Q  P  R  O  S  C  R  I  B  E  P  T  Y  T  Q  W  P  I
```

| | | | | |
|---|---|---|---|---|
| acumen | derogatory | impudent | prosperity | trenchant |
| adulation | effrontery | maelstrom | protean | trilateral |
| approbation | egocentric | malleable | sanctimonious | truculent |
| arrogate | expiate | nonchalant | sanction | vicarious |
| ascetic | impinge | ostentatious | sanguine | vicissitude |
| deprecate | implacable | proscribe | succor | vilify |

Fill in the crossword puzzle with words from Units 13-15.

**Across:**
3. failing to keep in mind
8. strong and sharp
11. marked by precise accordance with details
12. originating where it is found
15. a relaxed, comfortable feeling
16. habitually reserved and uncommunicative
17. anything short-lived
19. express strong disapproval of
20. happen to

**Down:**
1. intended to deceive
2. keep from happening or arising
4. never done or known before
5. failing to make distinctions
6. someone who fights
7. believing that only the self exists
9. tendency to believe readily
10. the state of nonexistence
13. lacking powers of invention
14. a small or moderate amount
18. remote in manner

# Lesson 105

Units 7-9 Review

Unscramble your vocabulary words.

NAXETT

still in existence

_____

EPLIOCM

of or involving dispute or controversy

_____

ISUAUOSSD

marked by care and persistent effort

_____

UCVSSIO

having a relatively high resistance to flow

_____

ERMDUBTAA

describe roughly or briefly

_____

TCCURENIVM

beat through cleverness and wit

_____

URCISOLUSR

expressing offensive reproach

_____

CDTCASIEE

lacking vitality or spirit; lifeless

_____

SOEISPNAR

a disparaging remark

_____

(continued on the next page)

O S O P N A E E R U E T M X _____
with little or no preparation or forethought

B U J L T A I N _____
joyful and proud especially because of triumph or success

I E A L A T P L _____
lessen or try to lessen the seriousness or extent of

L V I U E E S _____
difficult to detect or grasp by the mind

R S I T U F E _____
supply or feed to fullness

P I D A O S H N U A _____
so thin as to transmit light; see-through

H R P L T A E O _____
extreme excess

T I U Q B U S O U I _____
being present everywhere at once

L A P D I L _____
lacking in vitality or interest

P S O R U F L E U U S _____
serving no useful purpose

N A C A A E P _____
hypothetical remedy for all ills or diseases

# Lesson 106 Unit 16

Here is your next vocabulary unit. Read each word and its definition. Use the space below each word to write a synonym, write a sentence containing the word, draw a picture, or use some other device to help you commit the definitions to memory. You will have a quiz in Lesson 110.

- **amicable** (adj) characterized by friendship and good will

- **benevolent** (adj) intending to show kindness; generous in providing aid to others

- **complement** (n) something added to embellish or make perfect; either of two parts that mutually complete each other; (v) make complete or perfect

- **cumbersome** (adj) difficult to handle or use especially because of size or weight; not elegant or graceful in expression

- **discredit** (n) the state of being held in low esteem; (v) cause to be distrusted or disbelieved; damage the reputation of

- **eradicate** (v) kill in large numbers; destroy completely, as if down to the roots

- **fatuous** (adj) extremely silly or stupid

Continue learning your vocabulary unit. Read each word and its definition. Use the space below each word to write a synonym, write a sentence containing the word, draw a picture, or use some other device to help you commit the definitions to memory.  You will have a quiz in Lesson 110.

- **hegemony** (n) the dominance or leadership of one social group or nation over others

- **indoctrinate** (v) teach doctrines to; teach uncritically

- **largess** (n) a gift or money given, usually ostentatiously; liberality in bestowing gifts

- **modify** (v) make less severe, harsh, or extreme; make different

- **obsolete** (adj) no longer in use

- **paucity** (n) an insufficient quantity or number

- **pretentious** (adj) making claim to or creating an appearance of importance or distinction; intended to attract notice and impress others

# Lesson 108

Finish learning your vocabulary unit. Read each word and its definition. Use the space below each word to write a synonym, write a sentence containing the word, draw a picture, or use some other device to help you commit the definitions to memory.  You will have a quiz in Lesson 110.

- **quagmire** (n) a soft, wet area of low-lying land that sinks underfoot

- **reprove** (v) take to task; admonish

- **spontaneity** (n) the quality of acting without planning in advance

- **tactile** (adj) of or relating to the sense of touch; producing a sensation of touch

- **upbraid** (v) express criticism toward

- **whole** (n) all of something; (adj) including all components without exception; not injured or harmed; (adv) to a complete degree or to the full extent

# Lesson 109

Fill in the crossword puzzle with your vocabulary words. Study for your vocabulary quiz tomorrow. Make sure you know your words. Study ideas: read them out loud, copy the ones you are unsure of, have someone quiz you, use the words in conversation.

**Across:**
2. no longer in use
5. the state of being held in low esteem
6. an insufficient quantity or number
7. intended to attract notice and impress others
14. express criticism toward
17. teach uncritically
18. take to task
19. make complete or perfect
20. intending to show kindness

**Down:**
1. the dominance of one nation over others
3. liberality in bestowing gifts
4. characterized by friendship
8. kill in large numbers
9. all of something
10. the quality of acting without planning
11. not elegant or graceful in expression
12. producing a sensation of touch
13. a soft, wet area of low-lying land
15. make less severe
16. extremely silly or stupid

# Lesson 110

___

You can study your words before you take this quiz, but you MUST put them away before you take the quiz. Cheaters get ZERO points for their quiz. Check your answers and record your score on your grade sheet.

Circle the letter that contains the word that *best* fits.

1.  Peanut butter and apples _____ each other.

    a. discredit      b. modify      c. complement      d. indoctrinate

2.  The floppy disk I used to back up my school work is now _____.

    a. amicable      b. fatuous      c. cumbersome      d. obsolete

3.  A _____ learner prefers to be hands-on.

    a. tactile      b. pretentious      c. benevolent      d. whole

4. In a moment of complete _____, we drove to the next state just to have lunch.

    a. quagmire      b. spontaneity      c. hegemony      d. paucity

5.  We used vinegar to try to _____ the pungent odor.

    a. indoctrinate      b. reprove      c. upbraid      eradicate

Fill in the blank with the word that *best* fits.

6.  Being extremely silly or stupid is being _____.

7.  The dominance of one nation over others is _____.

8.  Creating an appearance of importance is being _____.

9.  To express criticism toward is to _____.

10.  A synonym for *change* might be _____.

Here is your next vocabulary unit. Read each word and its definition. Use the space below each word to write a synonym, write a sentence containing the word, draw a picture, or use some other device to help you commit the definitions to memory.  You will have a quiz in Lesson 115.

- **anachronism** (n) something located at a time when it could not have existed or occurred

- **blandish** (v) praise somewhat dishonestly

- **comply** (v) act in accordance with someone's rules, commands, or wishes

- **cupidity** (n) extreme greed for material wealth; avarice; covetousness

- **discrepancy** (n) a difference between conflicting facts or claims or opinions; an event that departs from expectations

- **eschew** (v) avoid and stay away from deliberately; stay clear of

- **fecund** (adj) capable of producing offspring or vegetation; intellectually productive

Continue learning your vocabulary unit. Read each word and its definition. Use the space below each word to write a synonym, write a sentence containing the word, draw a picture, or use some other device to help you commit the definitions to memory. You will have a quiz in Lesson 115.

- **heinous** (adj) extremely wicked; deeply criminal

- **ineffable** (adj) defying expression or description; too sacred to be uttered

- **latent** (adj) potentially existing but not presently evident or realized

- **momentous** (adj) of great significance

- **obstreperous** (adj) noisily and stubbornly defiant; boisterously and noisily aggressive

- **pejorative** (adj) expressing disapproval

- **primeval** (adj) having existed from the beginning; in an earliest or original state

# Lesson 113                                     Unit 17

Finish learning your vocabulary unit. Read each word and its definition. Use the space below each word to write a synonym, write a sentence containing the word, draw a picture, or use some other device to help you commit the definitions to memory.  You will have a quiz in Lesson 115.

- **qualitative** (adj) involving distinguishing attributes

- **rescind** (v) cancel officially

- **spurious** (adj) ostensibly valid, but not actually valid; plausible but false; not what it appears to be

- **tantamount** (adj) being essentially equal to something

- **usurp** (v) seize and take control without authority and possibly with force; take the place of

- **winsome** (adj) charming in a childlike or naïve way

# Lesson 114

Find your vocabulary words in the word search. As you find each one, repeat its definition. Look it up if you can't remember it. Study for your vocabulary quiz tomorrow. Make sure you know your words. Study ideas: read them out loud, copy the ones you are unsure of, have someone quiz you, use the words in conversation.

```
P K J N M Q B Q C Q A D Z K U V J B Y Y E P X P
M B E G Z S D H L P Z O T S F H O R J B K Y Y A
F C W H D R G U B T V F D W S T G J Y U F N L L
I C E V I T A T I L A U Q I D D N U C E F P P Q
E L B A F F E N I C Y L D Z Y Q I A R Z L T M S
G M C U P I D I T Y A N U L B S N T F O H P O L
L H R A N P R L E V A X C W A A U I L S S T C N
S Z H R Z I S X E L T B T F C T J O M E H V E R
R C A K R U J M B B N N U H Q U E A N F B X C L
Z D I B S U I F X E U D R I E I A N E I G Y W D
I L S X G R R U O O S O W Z V S P E T V E U H T
N J G J P W B D M U N K M O T B C K U O T H M L
D I L S C E D A O I M W M J L Z X H P A L K J U
U E Z C Q T T T S U L W M U J J M M E T K N Z R
X V E U N N M D P X M N V G S U T E W E X I K
S I E D A E W S L M J I F C B W D S G K U B Y X
L T G T M I X W Z O P A H A A E T D J L Q N Y H
H A O O D Y C N A P E R C S I D N I C S E R A L
L R M E W L M M T L W Q P Q N O G L M Z O D U D
X O N E A S U O R E P E R T S B O X X U I S C V
W J R L Y L Z V V N D K F F Z Y J I J D U K H S
T E L O Z A J W U E M Z X F F B L F K R Y W K Z
S P W I H Y U Q E E M O S N I W Q E P J A O P E
T G Y L J L T X G U U D B B S U O I R U P S D X
```

| | | | |
|---|---|---|---|
| anachronism | eschew | momentous | rescind |
| blandish | fecund | obstreperous | spurious |
| comply | heinous | pejorative | tantamount |
| cupidity | ineffable | primeval | usurp |
| discrepancy | latent | qualitative | winsome |

# Lesson 115

You can study your words before you take this quiz, but you MUST put them away before you take the quiz. Cheaters get ZERO points for their quiz. Check your answers and record your score on your grade sheet.

Circle the letter that contains the word that *best* fits.

1. It's hard to _____ with my doctor's orders of no food after 6 p.m.

    a. blandish       b. comply       c. eschew       d. rescind

2. Another word for cancel is _____.

    a. cupidity       b. anachronism       c. rescind       d. usurp

3. My dad's request was _____ to a demand.

    a. winsome       b. spurious       c. fecund       d. tantamount

4. The toddler became _____ after missing her nap.

    a. latent       b. obstreperous       c. pejorative       d. qualitative

5. A synonym for *avoid*.

    a. blandish       b. rescind       c. eschew       d. usurp

Fill in the blank with the word that *best* fits.

6. Charming in a childlike way is _____.

7. Plausible but false is _____.

8. Someone who is intellectually productive is _____.

9. Extremely wicked: _____.

10. Defying expression or description: _____.

Here is your next vocabulary unit. Read each word and its definition. Use the space below each word to write a synonym, write a sentence containing the word, draw a picture, or use some other device to help you commit the definitions to memory. You will have a quiz in Lesson 120.

- **anachronistic** (adj) chronologically misplaced

- **bolster** (n) a pillow put across a bed underneath the regular pillows; (v) support and strengthen; add padding to

- **compromise** (n) a middle way between two extremes; (v) arrive at a middle way between two extremes; expose or make liable to danger

- **cursory** (adj) hasty and without attention to detail; not thorough

- **discursive** (adj) proceeding to a conclusion by reason or argument rather than intuition; tending to depart from the main point or cover a wide range of subjects

- **estrange** (v) remove from customary environment or associations; arouse hostility or indifference in where there had formerly been love, affection, or friendliness

- **feign** (v) make believe with the intent to deceive; make a presence of

Continue learning your vocabulary unit. Read each word and its definition. Use the space below each word to write a synonym, write a sentence containing the word, draw a picture, or use some other device to help you commit the definitions to memory. You will have a quiz in Lesson 120.

- **hitherto** (adv) used in negative statement to describe a situation that has existed up to this point or up to the present time

- **inevitable** (n) an unavoidable event; (adj) incapable of being avoided or prevented; invariably occurring or appearing

- **latter** (n) the second of two or the second mentioned of two; (adj) referring to the second of two things or persons mentioned (or the last one or ones of several)

- **morass** (n) a soft, wet area of low-lying land that sinks underfoot; mire

- **obstruct** (v) hinder or prevent the progress or accomplishment of; block passage through; shut out from view

- **pellucid** (adj) transmitting light; able to be seen through with clarity; easily understandable

- **principled** (adj) based on or manifesting objectively defined standards of rightness or morality

Finish learning your vocabulary unit. Read each word and its definition. Use the space below each word to write a synonym, write a sentence containing the word, draw a picture, or use some other device to help you commit the definitions to memory. You will have a quiz in Lesson 120.

- **quantitative** (adj) relating to measurement of amount

- **resilient** (adj) recovering readily from adversity, depression, or the like; rebounds readily

- **staid** (adj) characterized by dignity and propriety

- **tedious** (adj) so lacking in interest as to cause mental weariness; using or containing too many words

- **utopia** (n) ideally perfect state; an imaginary place considered to be perfect or ideal

- **wistful** (adj) showing pensive sadness

Unscramble your vocabulary words. Study for your vocabulary quiz tomorrow. Make sure you know your words. Study ideas: read them out loud, copy the ones you are unsure of, have someone quiz you, use the words in conversation.

R N S O C T H C I A I A N

chronologically misplaced

_____

T P A U O I

ideally perfect state

_____

L I I R E P D C P N

based on or manifesting objectively defined standards of rightness or morality

_____

I O H R T H T E

a situation that has existed up to this point or up to the present time

_____

C I D U L P E L

transmitting light; able to be seen through with clarity; easily understandable

_____

E L T R A T

the second of two or the second mentioned of two

_____

G E N F I

make believe with the intent to deceive

_____

R U C Y S R O

hasty and without attention to detail

_____

I A E T V B E N L I

incapable of being avoided or prevented

_____

(continued on the next page)

**SRUTCTBO** _____

hinder or prevent the progress or accomplishment of

**RMOSSA** _____

a soft, wet area of low-lying land that sinks underfoot

**IATDS** _____

characterized by dignity and propriety

**STAREEGN** _____

remove from customary environment or associations

**TULISFW** _____

showing pensive sadness

**EATIUVTTINAQ** _____

relating to measurement of amount

**IENTERLIS** _____

recovering readily from adversity, depression, or the like

**ICUERIDSVS** _____

tending to depart from the main point or cover a wide range of subjects

**ISTOEUD** _____

so lacking in interest as to cause mental weariness

**ROSIMEPCMO** _____

a middle way between two extremes

**SEBTRLO** _____

support and strengthen; add padding to

You can study your words before you take this quiz, but you MUST put them away before you take the quiz. Cheaters get ZERO points for their quiz. Check your answers and record your score on your grade sheet.

Circle the letter that contains the word that *best* fits.

1.  The babbling brook and the shade of the trees made for a sort of _____.

    a. bolster       b. discursive        c. utopia        d. latter

2.  The road closure was _____ once the flooding rains began to fall.

    a. inevitable       b. pellucid        c. quantitative        d. staid

3.  Taking the nails out of the fence was a(n) _____ job.

    a. anachronistic        b. principled        c. wistful        d. tedious

4. The fence between us helped to _____ my courage as I met my first lion.

    a. compromise        b. bolster        c. estrange        d. feign

5.  A synonym for *mire*.

    a. utopia        b. morass        c. cursory        d. obstruct

Fill in the blank with the word that *best* fits.

6.  Something able to be seen through with clarity is _____.

7.  To hinder or prevent progress is to _____.

8.  Someone who recovers readily from adversity is _____.

9.  Characterized by dignity and propriety: _____.

10.  To make believe with the intent to deceive is to _____.

# Lesson 121                    Units 16-18 Review

Look over all of your words and notes from Units 16-18. Go over any rough spots in your memory.

# Lesson 122                    Units 16-18 Review

Find a partner to help you with this review game. See if you can guess the vocabulary word in ten guesses or less. Guess letters one at a time for each word and have your partner fill them in or let you know they're not in the word.

_ _ _ _ _ _ _ _ _ _ _
Hint: kill in large numbers

_ _ _ _ _ _ _ _
Hint: make less severe

_ _ _ _ _ _ _ _
Hint: intellectually productive

_ _ _ _ _ _ _ _
Hint: extremely wicked

_ _ _ _ _ _ _ _ _ _
Hint: of great significance

_ _ _ _ _ _
Hint: all of something

_ _ _ _ _ _ _ _ _
Hint: arouse hostility where there was affection

_ _ _ _ _ _ _
Hint: ideally perfect state

_ _ _ _ _ _ _ _ _
Hint: block passage through

_ _ _ _ _
Hint: take the place of

# Lesson 123

Match the word to its definition.

1. cursory      _____ extremely silly or stupid

2. fatuous      _____ express criticism toward

3. anachronism      _____ tending to depart from the main point

4. obstreperous      _____ able to be seen through with clarity

5. discursive      _____ plausible but false

6. morass      _____ hasty and without attention to detail

7. hegemony      _____ defying expression or description

8. upbraid      _____ the dominance of one social group over others

9. cupidity      _____ liberality in bestowing gifts

10. pellucid      _____ noisily and stubbornly defiant

11. pejorative      _____ characterized by dignity and propriety

12. ineffable      _____ expressing disapproval

13. largess      _____ something located at a time when it couldn't have existed

14. paucity      _____ an insufficient quantity or number

15. eschew      _____ avoid and stay away from deliberately

16. spurious      _____ a soft, wet area of low-lying land that sinks underfoot

17. staid      _____ extreme greed for material wealth

# Lesson 124

Can you find all 60 of your vocabulary words in this massive word search? Flip back through your three units for the word list if you need it.

```
P P R N D J M A Y D Q U F J K C P M N W D C U P I D I T Y H
G R Q K D O U X D P U C U C O M P R O M I S E H J S F A H E
H I M F X M P D Q H A D E C P R I N C I P L E D H F S D V G
E M O B S O L E T E L E G W J Q M Q E V O K Z C W E G Y V E
I E O I N D O C T R I N A T E D F G B W I S T F U L I K Y M
N V M Z H I T H E R T O P E L L U C I D P N I X V Z J K O
O A X W K V G K B B A T F R E A M U A N A C H R O N I S M N
U L L T U P R V L G T F U X Z J M O J M M R E G D Q U C N Y
S V G W V I O P A Z I T R E S I L I E N T O J C U R S O R Y
B E N E V O L E N T V F T P S J C K C Z B O L S T E R O W V
C M N H P F Q E D Z E E K A P S M F O A D I S C R E D I T P
O A W W L R Y W I L F I X U U U D P G A B I N E F F A B L E
M H P I V P B G S J Z G M C R H A R W Z S L R H U Y V I M S
P C J L K S C V H H Z N O I I B V E T I A P E Q S M Z F S X
L F T B T A N T A M O U N T O A K T Q P N F A T U O U S N S
Y T E D I O U S X O L A O Y U N C E S P F S K T A C T I L E
Q U A N T I T A T I V E Z S S A U N O E D A O S S D I P X F
U R Y U H U M T G G K R J A X C M T B J Q I W M Y D L C C B
A E U P E F O A S L E A L E J H B I S O L O S Z E I A G P H
G S T B K O M J T A A D A S K R E O T R M P Q C W S R R R W
M C O R V B E A G T J I T H L O R U R A O A I J U C G S E K
I I P A J S N E J T L C E N P N S S E T R J N Z M R E T P W
R N I I T T T D K E U A N C T I O W P I A U E Z O E S A R H
E D A D S R O L B R E T T R X S M T E V S S V F D P S I O O
Y E J F G U U E S C H E W Q O T E N R E S U I E I A B D V L
J K Y U E C S S P O N T A N E I T Y O O Y R T C F N C J E E
C W L E G T N Z I D W Y R P T C R P U T R P A U Y C V W J N
Q C O M P L E M E N T S Z V E J G T S N V K B N B Y X O Q X
J V H R V Q A G E S T R A N G E M N Z S X N L D L G V D P Q
S R F U K F B W C E X V U F E U R W N U V G E L O C F H X K
```

# Lesson 125                    Units 16-18 Review Quiz

If you got 100% on all three of your vocabulary quizzes so far, no vocab for you today. Way to go! If you didn't, take this review quiz. If you score higher on this than you did on one of your previous quizzes, you may replace the grade of one of those quizzes on your grade sheet (just one).

Circle the letter that contains the word that *best* fits.

1.  The desire to belong is a _____ one.

    a. qualitative      b. primeval      c.  tedious      d. pretentious

2.  The _____ box was hard to get through the door.

    a. tactile      b. latent      c. cumbersome      d. resilient

3. As _____ as it sounds, I prefer dining at country clubs.

    a. pretentious      b. obsolete      c. quantitative      d. anachronistic

4. The _____ clothing ruined the movie for me.

    a. anachronistic      b. wistful      c. tantamount      d. benevolent

5. My sister tried to _____ sickness to get out of doing chores.

    a. rescind      b. feign      c. complement      d. discredit

Fill in the blank with the word that *best* fits.

6.  Something that is no longer in use is _____.

7.  To cancel officially is to _____.

8.  To support and strengthen is to _____.

9.  Being generous in providing aid to others is being _____.

10.  An unavoidable event is _____.

# Lesson 126 {#header} Unit 19

Here is your next vocabulary unit. Read each word and its definition. Use the space below each word to write a synonym, write a sentence containing the word, draw a picture, or use some other device to help you commit the definitions to memory. You will have a quiz in Lesson 130.

- **analyze** (v) consider in detail to discover essential features or meaning; break down into components

- **boon** (n) a desirable state; (adj) very close and convivial

- **concomitant** (n) an event or situation that happens at the same time as or in connection with another; (adj) occurring with or following as a consequence

- **debilitate** (v) make weak

- **disdain** (n) lack of respect accompanied by a feeling of dislike; (v) look down on; reject with contempt

- **evanescent** (adj) tending to vanish like vapor

- **feral** (adj) wild and menacing

Continue learning your vocabulary unit. Read each word and its definition. Use the space below each word to write a synonym, write a sentence containing the word, draw a picture, or use some other device to help you commit the definitions to memory. You will have a quiz in Lesson 130.

- **hypothesis** (n) a proposal intended to explain certain facts or observations; an educated guess; an opinion based on incomplete evidence

- **inexorable** (adj) not to be placated or appeased or moved by entreaty; impervious to pleas, persuasion, requests, reason

- **lax** (adj) lacking in rigor or strictness; lacking in firmness or tension

- **multifarious** (adj) having many aspects or qualities

- **obtuse** (adj) an angle between 90 and 180 degrees; lacking insight or discernment; slow to learn or understand

- **pensive** (adj) deeply or seriously thoughtful; showing sadness

- **probity** (n) complete and confirmed integrity; having strong moral principles

# Lesson 128 Unit 19

Finish learning your vocabulary unit. Read each word and its definition. Use the space below each word to write a synonym, write a sentence containing the word, draw a picture, or use some other device to help you commit the definitions to memory. You will have a quiz in Lesson 130.

- **quasi** (adj) having some resemblance

- **restive** (adj) being in a tense state; impatient especially under restriction or delay

- **static** (n) a crackling or hissing noise caused by electrical interference; angry criticism; (adj) not in physical motion; showing little if any change

- **tenacious** (adj) good at remembering; stubbornly unyielding; sticking together

- **vacuous** (adj) devoid of intelligence or thought; devoid of significance or force; devoid of matter

- **wizened** (adj) lean and wrinkled by shrinkage as from age or illness

# Lesson 129

Unit 19 Practice

Fill in the crossword puzzle with your vocabulary words. Study for your vocabulary quiz tomorrow. Make sure you know your words. Study ideas: read them out loud, copy the ones you are unsure of, have someone quiz you, use the words in conversation.

**Across:**
2. break down into components
4. deeply or seriously thoughtful
11. make weak
12. slow to learn or understand
14. having many aspects or qualities
17. wild and menacing
18. stubbornly unyielding
19. complete and confirmed integrity
20. lean and wrinkled by shrinkage as from age or illness

**Down:**
1. having some resemblance
3. tending to vanish like vapor
5. devoid of intelligence or thought
6. an educated guess
7. not in physical motion
8. impervious to reason
9. lacking in rigor or strictness
10. occurring with
13. very close and convivial
15. being in a tense state
16. look down on

# Lesson 130

# Unit 19 Quiz

You can study your words before you take this quiz, but you MUST put them away before you take the quiz. Cheaters get ZERO points for their quiz. Check your answers and record your score on your grade sheet.

Circle the letter that contains the word that *best* fits.

1.  I enjoy the _____ sensations of hot apple pie and frigid vanilla ice cream.

    a. feral      b. inexorable      c. vacuous      d. concomitant

2.  Her face was _____ by age.

    a. quasi      b. wizened      c. evanescent      d. boon

3.  The _____ people and traditions are what make America great.

    a. evanescent      b. multifarious      c. lax      d. quasi

4. The brisk breeze was a _____ to the sweaty sailors.

    a. boon      b. hypothesis      c. static      d. probity

5.  The _____ recession hit the small business sector hard.

    a. pensive      b. obtuse      c. tenacious      d. lax

Fill in the blank with the word that *best* fits.

6.  A cat that is not a house pet might be considered _____.

7.  Complete and confirmed integrity is _____.

8.  Something that tends to vanish like vapor is _____.

9.  _____ is a crackling noise caused by electrical interference.

10.  An educated guess is a(n) _____.

Here is your next vocabulary unit. Read each word and its definition. Use the space below each word to write a synonym, write a sentence containing the word, draw a picture, or use some other device to help you commit the definitions to memory.  You will have a quiz in Lesson 135.

- **anarchy** (n) a state of lawlessness and disorder

- **brusque** (adj) marked by rude or peremptory shortness

- **concurrent** (adj) occurring or operating at the same time

- **decry** (v) express strong disapproval of

- **dissemble** (v) make believe with the intent to deceive; hide under a false appearance; behave unnaturally

- **evince** (v) give expression to

- **fetid** (adj) offensively malodorous; foul; smelly

# Lesson 132 Unit 20

Continue learning your vocabulary unit. Read each word and its definition. Use the space below each word to write a synonym, write a sentence containing the word, draw a picture, or use some other device to help you commit the definitions to memory. You will have a quiz in Lesson 135.

- **hypothetical** (n) an imagined possibility, circumstance, statement, situation, etc.; (adj) based primarily on surmise rather than adequate evidence

- **informal** (adj) not done in accordance with rules or convention; not officially recognized or controlled

- **legerdemain** (n) an illusory feat; considered magical by naïve observers

- **mundane** (adj) found in the ordinary course of events; belonging to this earth or world - not ideal or heavenly

- **odious** (adj) unequivocally detestable

- **penurious** (adj) not having enough money to pay for necessities; excessively unwilling to spend

- **proclivity** (n) a natural inclination

Finish learning your vocabulary unit. Read each word and its definition. Use the space below each word to write a synonym, write a sentence containing the word, draw a picture, or use some other device to help you commit the definitions to memory.  You will have a quiz in Lesson 135.

- **quay** (n) wharf usually built parallel to the shoreline

- **restrained** (v) restricted so as to make free movement difficult; prevented the action of; (adj) cool and formal in manner; marked by avoidance of extravagance or extremes

- **stolid** (adj) having or revealing little emotion or sensibility; not easily aroused or excited

- **tenuous** (adj) very thin; lacking substance or significance

- **validate** (v) give evidence for; confirm the soundness of

- **zealot** (n) a fervent and even militant proponent of something

# Lesson 134

Find your vocabulary words in the word search. As you find each one, repeat its definition. Look it up if you can't remember it. Study for your vocabulary quiz tomorrow. Make sure you know your words. Study ideas: read them out loud, copy the ones you are unsure of, have someone quiz you, use the words in conversation.

```
J  V  V  P  R  I  T  T  G  I  H  L  G  B  J  P  V  D  E  L  B
S  P  C  P  Z  A  B  N  T  L  V  Y  K  Q  U  A  Y  C  X  E  X
G  R  I  S  G  X  Z  H  O  B  T  A  E  A  J  T  N  O  X  G  V
L  C  N  Z  H  C  Q  Y  Y  I  M  S  L  X  K  I  X  A  V  E  F
L  D  L  K  T  X  M  E  V  P  P  G  H  I  V  R  U  Q  U  R  E
D  V  V  K  S  K  N  I  V  T  O  E  H  E  D  P  Z  Q  N  D  T
I  B  F  Z  D  A  L  Q  O  F  N  T  N  N  U  A  S  C  V  E  I
S  J  I  P  D  C  F  L  A  A  C  D  H  U  Q  U  T  T  S  M  D
S  O  H  N  O  O  A  T  A  C  N  O  V  E  R  S  B  E  O  A  I
E  O  U  R  M  E  D  Y  E  L  W  A  N  B  T  I  Q  W  J  I  Q
M  M  P  N  Z  P  R  I  A  N  D  E  R  C  E  I  O  M  Z  N  G
B  S  S  Y  N  C  D  M  O  Y  U  C  T  C  U  Q  C  U  O  J  D
L  A  B  O  E  I  R  X  S  U  T  O  X  X  H  R  Y  A  S  F  M
E  N  L  D  L  O  F  U  W  Q  S  N  U  M  R  Y  R  Q  L  H  T
J  V  B  O  F  E  B  I  D  H  C  J  Q  S  J  J  R  E  E  K  Q
I  C  T  N  A  L  R  E  S  T  R  A  I  N  E  D  F  W  N  Y  A
I  S  I  S  K  H  K  S  I  G  O  J  W  U  B  D  Z  G  R  T  M
X  B  T  U  M  I  D  X  T  Q  V  D  U  T  Q  W  A  Q  D  G  X
O  B  J  D  E  G  E  E  Z  K  M  N  G  M  A  M  H  L  Y  M  U
A  K  X  S  S  R  O  N  S  Z  L  B  U  S  P  F  B  T  Z  U  L
V  V  Y  N  E  C  J  V  M  L  N  O  V  P  C  G  G  Z  C  Z  J
```

| | | | |
|---|---|---|---|
| anarchy | evince | mundane | restrained |
| brusque | fetid | odious | stolid |
| concurrent | hypothetical | penurious | tenuous |
| decry | informal | proclivity | validate |
| dissemble | legerdemain | quay | zealot |

# Lesson 135                                               Unit 20 Quiz

You can study your words before you take this quiz, but you MUST put them away before you take the quiz. Cheaters get ZERO points for their quiz. Check your answers and record your score on your grade sheet.

Circle the letter that contains the word that *best* fits.

1.  Many lived a(n) _____ existence after the Great Depression.

      a. concurrent    b. informal    c. penurious    d. quay

2.  A synonym for *foul* could be _____.

      a. fetid    b. brusque    c. stolid    d. tenuous

3.  His _____ personality meant he had very few friends.

      a. informal    b. odious    c. zealot    d. legerdemain

4. The toddler had a _____ to misbehave.

      a. gargoyle    b. dissemble    c. anarchy    d. proclivity

5. I hope my children _____ an attitude of compassion for others.

      a. evince    b. decry    c. restrained    d. validate

Fill in the blank with the word that *best* fits.

6.  Another word for "slight of hand" is _____.

7.  A wharf usually built parallel to the shoreline is a(n) _____.

8.  Someone who displays very little emotion is _____.

9.  A state of lawlessness and disorder is known as _____.

10.  Things that occur at the same time are _____.

# Lesson 136

# Unit 21

Here is your next vocabulary unit. Read each word and its definition. Use the space below each word to write a synonym, write a sentence containing the word, draw a picture, or use some other device to help you commit the definitions to memory. You will have a quiz in Lesson 140.

- **anathema** (n) a detested person or thing

- **buffet** (n) a meal at which guests help themselves; (v) strike against forcefully; beat repeatedly

- **condescending** (v) behaving in a patronizing manner; acting in an undignified way; (adj) characteristic of those who treat others in a patronizing manner

- **defile** (v) place under suspicion or cast doubt upon; make dirty or spotty; spot, stain, or pollute

- **disseminate** (v) cause to become widely known

- **exacerbate** (v) make worse; exasperate or irritate

- **fleeting** (v) moving along rapidly and lightly; (adj) lasting for a markedly brief time

Continue learning your vocabulary unit. Read each word and its definition. Use the space below each word to write a synonym, write a sentence containing the word, draw a picture, or use some other device to help you commit the definitions to memory. You will have a quiz in Lesson 140.

- **iconoclast** (n) a destroyer of images used in religious worship; someone who attacks cherished ideas or traditional institutions

- **ingenuous** (adj) characterized by an inability to mask your feelings; not devious; lacking in sophistication or worldliness

- **lethargic** (adj) deficient in alertness or activity

- **munificence** (n) liberality in bestowing gifts; generosity of spirit

- **officious** (adj) intrusive in a meddling or offensive manner

- **perfidious** (adj) tending to betray

- **procrastinate** (v) postpone doing what one should be doing

Finish learning your vocabulary unit. Read each word and its definition. Use the space below each word to write a synonym, write a sentence containing the word, draw a picture, or use some other device to help you commit the definitions to memory. You will have a quiz in Lesson 140.

- **quixotic** (adj) not sensible about practical matters; idealistic and unrealistic

- **retorted** (v) answered back

- **strenuous** (adj) characterized by or performed with much energy or force; taxing to the utmost

- **timorous** (adj) timid by nature or revealing timidity

- **vapid** (adj) lacking taste or flavor; lacking significance or liveliness of spirit

- **zenith** (n) the point above the observer that is directly opposite the nadir; the highest point

# Lesson 139

Unscramble your vocabulary words. Study for your vocabulary quiz tomorrow. Make sure you know your words. Study ideas: read them out loud, copy the ones you are unsure of, have someone quiz you, use the words in conversation.

**E T F B F U**
strike against forcefully; beat repeatedly

_____

**O N I S C L A O C T**
someone who attacks cherished ideas or traditional institutions

_____

**F F I O I U O C S**
intrusive in a meddling or offensive manner

_____

**C B R X E E A T A E**
make worse; exasperate or irritate

_____

**E N I I C N C U M E F**
liberality in bestowing gifts; generosity of spirit

_____

**U T Q I O C X I**
not sensible about practical matters; idealistic and unrealistic

_____

**I E F E D L**
spot, stain, or pollute

_____

**H A A M A N E T**
a detested person or thing

_____

**R E A C P T N S A R I O T**
postpone doing what one should be doing

_____

(continued on the next page)

O D R T T E E R
answered back
_____

I N T E H Z
the highest point
_____

U D R S I F O E I P
tending to betray
_____

U E T S R O U S N
taxing to the utmost
_____

I A T M S I N E D E S
cause to become widely known
_____

N E D S D G E I N C C O N
behaving in a patronizing manner
_____

N U E O I U N G S
characterized by an inability to mask your feelings
_____

R M T U I O S O
timid by nature or revealing timidity
_____

A V P D I
lacking significance or liveliness of spirit
_____

H R L A I E T G C
deficient in alertness or activity
_____

G E T E F L N I
lasting for a markedly brief time
_____

# Lesson 140                                    Unit 21 Quiz

You can study your words before you take this quiz, but you MUST put them away before you take the quiz. Cheaters get ZERO points for their quiz. Check your answers and record your score on your grade sheet.

Circle the letter that contains the word that *best* fits.

1.   The waves continued to _____ the side of the boat in the storm.

    a. buffet    b. defile    c. procrastinate    d. disseminate

2.   After the large meal, we were all feeling a bit _____.

    a. ingenuous    b. fleeting    c. lethargic    d. officious

3.  Her _____ was widely known among the local charities.

    a. anathema    b. munificence    c. iconoclast    d. zenith

4. The_____ entertainment did not keep our attention.

    a. vapid    b. timorous    c. strenuous    d. perfidious

5.  A synonym for *replied*.

    a. procrastinate    b. exacerbate    c. retorted    d. disseminate

Fill in the blank with the word that *best* fits.

6.  A detested person or thing is a(n) _____.

7. Tending to betray: _____.

8. Something that is extremely taxing is _____.

9. To cause to become widely known is to _____.

10.  Someone who attacks cherished ideas is a(n) _____.

# Lesson 141          Units 19-21 Review

Look over all of your words and notes from Units 19-21. Go over any rough spots in your memory.

# Lesson 142          Units 19-21 Review

Find a partner to help you with this review game. See if you can guess the vocabulary word in ten guesses or less. Guess letters one at a time for each word and have your partner fill them in or let you know they're not in the word.

— — — — — — — —          — — — — — —

Hint: excessively unwilling to spend          Hint: slow to learn

— — — — — — —          — — — — — — —

Hint: give expression to          Hint: look down on

— — — — — — — — —          — — — — —

Hint: deficient in alertness          Hint: wild

— — — — — — — —          — — — — — —

Hint: detested person or thing          Hint: make dirty

— — — — — — — —          — — — — —

Hint: give evidence for          Hint: having some resemblance

# Lesson 143                                    Units 19-21 Review

Match the word to its definition.

1. buffet          _____ a natural inclination

2. quixotic        _____ tending to betray

3. proclivity      _____ complete and confirmed integrity

4. tenuous         _____ timid by nature

5. debilitate      _____ idealistic and unrealistic

6. inexorable      _____ lacking in taste or flavor

7. evanescent      _____ tending to vanish like vapor

8. probity         _____ marked by rude or peremptory shortness

9. stolid          _____ beat repeatedly

10. perfidious     _____ deeply or seriously thoughtful

11. vapid          _____ an illusory feat

12. dissemble      _____ lacking substance or significance

13. pensive        _____ not easily aroused or excited

14. brusque        _____ liberality in bestowing gifts

15. legerdemain    _____ make weak

16. munificence    _____ hide under a false appearance

17. timorous       _____ impervious to pleas or reason

# Lesson 144

Can you find all 60 of your vocabulary words in this massive word search? Flip back through your three units for the word list if you need it.

```
U L I N G E N U O U S I V L G H U H K E D I S D A I N S I I
M J Z J Z P H H O H H R H W Q Z Y L R A N M Q C L H D D U X
N U L T O V W I Z E N E D M S K Z C Z E A L O T K B P L B R
D A X Q R B F A S T R E N U O U S J Q A Z P T G H S Z Q H E
I P O B T U S E T P R O C R A S T I N A T E D R R W G U J S
I M I T E N A C I O U S E T Q R C O N C O M I T A N T X D T
Q O Q K P E R F I D I O U S M R U C P C F Q S Y H X J B J R
H G A A G N L U D V B R U S Q U E W E F E A S K V E R Z J A
G O I C O N O C L A S T I O B K V J N E R Y E L M Z F A T I
F K W U X P P M W J Q E L R J V A H S V A F M C X Q R V R N
B E Z E N I T H T Q T F J T M V L Q I I L C I Z W X Q J B E
U R T L O C O N C U R R E N T A I Q V N T Q N L F W X I M D
F I Z I R M C O W A G B K R X P D U E C X T A V A C U O U S
F Z Y U D C W Y T S Z S A M N I A A C E L E T H A R G I C Y
E G V P V O M O T I U C A I U D T Y X H J C E V I M P B G J
T S T B M N O U H D Y U P O N N E N H Y P O T H E T I C A L
B E Y D U D D V L L E X F R D F I E X A C E R B A T E A T U
U D Q W N E I V Q T E F X Z O P O F L D X W R K B C R N X P
R D U N D S O J Z Q I G I M D C R R I T I M O R O U S A A E
E E I D A C U T M U H F E L A H L T M C X R P L U L R L N N
T B X I N E S F G E I S A R E L Y I Z A E K H A O D E Y A U
O I O S E N P O V V I N T R D T R P V U L N E X Z B S Z T R
R L T S Y D R F T A G S E O I E D I O I F R C X Z O T E H I
T I I E V I O F E N N O I X L O M S H T T L B E D O I X E O
E T C M Q N B I N E H Y T Y O I U A T H H Y E D X N V U M U
D A Y B L G I C U S D X A Z L R D S I A F E H E N U E F A S
J T M L O E T I O C N H J Q U L A T C N T K S J T Z K X C D
T E L E T L Y O U E C D E C R Y B B N N R I Z I C I Q K H O
H B L Z Z Q F U S N I D W T H J S P L H P S C H S J N V T L
A N A R C H Y S H T C U R A Y B M J F E U E M F R R K G H S
```

# Lesson 145                     Units 19-21 Review Quiz

If you got 100% on all three of your vocabulary quizzes so far, no vocab for you today. Way to go! If you didn't, take this review quiz. If you score higher on this than you did on one of your previous quizzes, you may replace the grade of one of those quizzes on your grade sheet (just one).

Circle the letter that contains the word that *best* fits.

1.  A synonym for *smelly*.

    a. multifarious      b. vacuous      c. officious      d. fetid

2.  The baby held my finger in his _____ little fist.

    a. tenacious      b. odious      c. ingenuous      d. strenuous

3.  If you _____ too much you'll miss out on our weekend plans.

    a. exacerbate      b. procrastinate      c. disseminate      d. decry

4. The _____ task of raking the leaves was somehow soothing to me.

    a. mundane      b. hypothetical      c. concurrent      d. wizened

5. Their _____ expressions told me it was time to end the lecture.

    a. multifarious      b. officious      c. vacuous      d. strenuous

Fill in the blank with the word that *best* fits.

6.  A state of lawlessness and disorder: _____.

7.  Having many aspects or qualities is known as _____.

8.  Something that's unequivocally detestable is _____.

9.  To cause to become widely known is to _____.

10.  The highest point is the _____.

# Lesson 146 Unit 22

Here is your next vocabulary unit. Read each word and its definition. Use the space below each word to write a synonym, write a sentence containing the word, draw a picture, or use some other device to help you commit the definitions to memory. You will have a quiz in Lesson 150.

- **anecdote** (n) short account of an incident

- **burgeon** (v) grow and flourish

- **condition** (n) a state at a particular time; a statement of what is required as part of an agreement; (v) put into a better state

- **deleterious** (adj) harmful to living things

- **dissident** (n) a person who dissents from some established policy; (adj) characterized by departure from accepted beliefs or standards; disagreeing, especially with a majority

- **exasperation** (n) actions that cause great irritation; feeling of great annoyance

- **florid** (adj) elaborately or excessively ornamented; inclined to a healthy reddish color often associated with outdoor life

Continue learning your vocabulary unit. Read each word and its definition. Use the space below each word to write a synonym, write a sentence containing the word, draw a picture, or use some other device to help you commit the definitions to memory. You will have a quiz in Lesson 150.

- **illicit** (adj) contrary to accepted morality; contrary to or forbidden by law

- **inherent** (adj) existing as an essential constituent or characteristic; in the nature of something though not readily apparent

- **licentious** (adj) lacking moral discipline; especially sexually unrestrained

- **myopic** (adj) unable to see distant objects clearly; lacking foresight or scope

- **omit** (v) prevent from being included or considered or accepted; leave undone or leave out

- **perfunctory** (adj) not thorough; done or produced as a formality only

- **proficient** (adj) having or showing knowledge and skill and aptitude

Finish learning your vocabulary unit. Read each word and its definition. Use the space below each word to write a synonym, write a sentence containing the word, draw a picture, or use some other device to help you commit the definitions to memory. You will have a quiz in Lesson 150.

- **rancor** (n) a feeling of deep and bitter anger and ill-will

- **reverence** (n) a feeling of profound respect for someone or something; (v) regard with feelings of respect; consider hallowed or exalted

- **stringent** (adj) demanding strict attention to rules and procedures

- **torpid** (adj) slow and apathetic; in a condition of biological rest or suspended animation

- **variable** (n) something subject to change; a quantity that can assume any of a set of values; (adj) liable to or capable of change; marked by diversity or difference

- **zephyr** (n) a slight wind, usually refreshing

Fill in the crossword puzzle with your vocabulary words. Study for your vocabulary quiz tomorrow. Make sure you know your words. Study ideas: read them out loud, copy the ones you are unsure of, have someone quiz you, use the words in conversation.

**Across:**
1. not thorough
6. short account of an incident
11. slow and apathetic
13. lacking foresight or scope
15. grow and flourish
18. existing as an essential characteristic
19. something subject to change
20. disagreeing, especially with a majority

**Down:**
2. feeling of great annoyance
3. a feeling of deep and bitter anger
4. elaborately or excessively ornamented
5. harmful to living things
7. consider hallowed or exalted
8. a slight wind, usually refreshing
9. demanding strict attention to rules
10. a state at a particular time
12. showing knowledge and skill
14. lacking moral discipline
16. leave undone or leave out
17. contrary to accepted morality

# Lesson 150                                    Unit 22 Quiz

You can study your words before you take this quiz, but you MUST put them away before you take the quiz. Cheaters get ZERO points for their quiz. Check your answers and record your score on your grade sheet.

Circle the letter that contains the word that *best* fits.

1.   Having a low level of vitamin D can be _____ to your health.

    a. deleterious    b. florid    c. illicit    d. proficient

2.   In late spring, the weeds in our yard _____ and take over if we don't tend to them.

    a. omit    b. condition    c. burgeon    d. reverence

3.  A synonym for immoral could be _____.

    a. florid    b. inherent    c. perfunctory    d. licentious

4. In my _____ I let out a huge sigh.

    a. zephyr    b. exasperation    c. anecdote    d. variable

5.  California is a state with _____ air pollution guidelines.

    a. torpid    b. stringent    c. perfunctory    d. myopic

Fill in the blank with the word that *best* fits.

6.  A feeling of deep and bitter anger and ill-will is _____.

7.  A short account of an incident is known as a(n) _____.

8.  Something slow and apathetic is _____.

9.  Something marked by diversity or difference _____.

10.  Elaborately or excessively ornamented is known as _____.

# Lesson 151 Unit 23

Here is your next vocabulary unit. Read each word and its definition. Use the space below each word to write a synonym, write a sentence containing the word, draw a picture, or use some other device to help you commit the definitions to memory. You will have a quiz in Lesson 155.

- **anonymous** (adj) having no known name or identity or source; lacking individuality

- **burnish** (n) the property of being smooth and shiny; (v) polish and make shiny

- **conditional** (adj) qualified by reservations

- **demagogue** (n) a political leader who seeks support by appealing to popular passions and prejudices

- **dither** (n) an excited state of agitation; (v) act nervously; be undecided; be uncertain; make a fuss; be agitated

- **exculpate** (v) pronounce not guilty of criminal charges

- **fortuitous** (adj) having no cause or apparent cause; occurring by a happy chance

Continue learning your vocabulary unit. Read each word and its definition. Use the space below each word to write a synonym, write a sentence containing the word, draw a picture, or use some other device to help you commit the definitions to memory. You will have a quiz in Lesson 155.

- **immense** (adj) unusually great in size, amount, degree, extent, or scope

- **inimical** (adj) not friendly

- **limpid** (adj) clear and bright; transmitting light; easily understandable (as in language)

- **myriad** (n) a large, indefinite number; (adj) too numerous to be counted

- **omnipotent** (adj) having unlimited power

- **perpetual** (adj) continuing forever or indefinitely; uninterrupted in time and indefinitely long continuing

- **prolific** (adj) intellectually productive; bearing in abundance especially offspring

Finish learning your vocabulary unit. Read each word and its definition. Use the space below each word to write a synonym, write a sentence containing the word, draw a picture, or use some other device to help you commit the definitions to memory.  You will have a quiz in Lesson 155.

- **rancorous** (adj) showing deep-seated resentment

- **ribald** (n) someone who uses vulgar and offensive language; (adj) humorously vulgar

- **stupefy** (v) make dull or muddle with drunkenness or infatuation; be a mystery or bewildering to; make senseless or dizzy

- **tractable** (adj) easily managed (controlled, taught, or molded); responsive to suggestions and influences

- **variegated** (v) changed the appearance of; made something diverse and varied; (adj) having a variety of colors

- **zest** (n) vigorous and enthusiastic enjoyment; a tart spicy quality; (v) add herbs or spices to

# Lesson 154

Find your vocabulary words in the word search. As you find each one, repeat its definition. Look it up if you can't remember it. Study for your vocabulary quiz tomorrow. Make sure you know your words. Study ideas: read them out loud, copy the ones you are unsure of, have someone quiz you, use the words in conversation.

```
K Q R Z E D T W I J C C M Y R I A D F G T I Y
O I T F R K I A S V F Z P X N J N U O R D I P
A Q C D F D K T Y P P H S O Q I B G R D K J P
Q N W V Q F K B H S U V A E D H G G T T R G M
J J O P K W X O Z E S T V N D J S E U O W N D
K A T N E Y R W H R R U I S Y J W W I H U E J
T X E R Y R C O N D I T I O N A L G T A X E Y
Z C T X A M P V W Z B E P A Z M I L O T U P D
V R I G C C O E U N K Q J P M X D T U X S E L
S F A M R U T U T E P R O L I F I C S S W Q U
I M N N M F L A S U B N I Y I S T U P E F Y O
I F L W C E A P B E A E S E O P Q Y U T T R M
H D Y M G O N C A L I L Y R N G C G I Z X S N
F F N Z G G R S M T E V I G V J O B I J H C I
Z Y D F K W Y O E N E Q L P K G H A A S C O P
Q O U J W E V Z U Z R N X A A W L R I A N C O
F C I R I I K O X S L L I M P I D N J S L J T
V A R I E G A T E D J G E W S Z R M I K Z J E
R N P B G E E R E G O D D G B U Z H N Z N R N
K D E A F L R U M M F Z P P B U E S L L X C T
F E M L I N R I L R W N L B K M A C T E Z I C
K K I D A Q K G W G I I N I M I C A L D E S F
Y U U O N M X E J T O O N G I T C M X L D I T
```

| anonymous | exculpate | myriad | ribald |
| burnish | fortuitous | omnipotent | stupefy |
| conditional | immense | perpetual | tractable |
| demagogue | inimical | prolific | variegated |
| dither | limpid | rancorous | zest |

You can study your words before you take this quiz, but you MUST put them away before you take the quiz. Cheaters get ZERO points for their quiz. Check your answers and record your score on your grade sheet.

Circle the letter that contains the word that *best* fits.

1.  The _____ tip helped the police find the missing car.

      a. conditional      b. inimical      c. anonymous      d. prolific

2.  A series of _____ circumstances helped advance his political career.

      a. fortuitous      b. rancorous      c. omnipotent      d. limpid

3.  A terrible and _____ argument erupted.

      a. conditional      b. variegated      c. tractable      d. rancorous

4. Alyssa rushed out of the room in an apparent _____.

      a. demagogue      b. dither      c. burnish      d. zest

5.  The headlights seemed to _____ the deer.

      a. stupefy      b. exculpate      c. zest      d. dither

Fill in the blank with the word that *best* fits.

6.  To polish and make shiny is to _____.

7.  To pronounce not guilty of criminal charges is to _____.

8.  Something that is clear and bright is _____.

9.  Continuing forever or indefinitely is known as _____.

10.  To make senseless or dizzy is to _____.

# Lesson 156 Unit 24

Here is your next vocabulary unit. Read each word and its definition. Use the space below each word to write a synonym, write a sentence containing the word, draw a picture, or use some other device to help you commit the definitions to memory. You will have a quiz in Lesson 160.

- **antagonist** (n) someone who offers opposition

- **buttress** (n) a support usually of stone or brick that supports the wall of a building; (v) to make stronger or defensible

- **condolence** (n) an expression of sympathy with another's grief

- **demean** (v) reduce in worth or character, usually verbally

- **divergent** (adj) moving apart from another or from a standard; tending to move apart in different directions

- **execrable** (adj) of very poor quality or condition; unequivocally detestable

- **fractious** (adj) stubbornly resistant to authority or control; easily irritated or annoyed; unpredictably difficult in operation

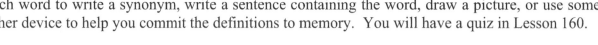

Continue learning your vocabulary unit. Read each word and its definition. Use the space below each word to write a synonym, write a sentence containing the word, draw a picture, or use some other device to help you commit the definitions to memory. You will have a quiz in Lesson 160.

- **imminent** (adj) close in time; about to occur

- **iniquity** (n) morally objectionable behavior; an unjust act

- **lobbyist** (n) someone who is employed to persuade legislators to vote for legislation that favors the lobbyist's employer

- **nadir** (n) an extreme state of adversity; the lowest point of anything

- **opportune** (adj) suitable or at a time that is suitable or advantageous, especially for a particular purpose

- **perplex** (v) be a mystery or bewildering to; make more complicated

- **promulgate** (v) state or announce; put a law into effect by formal declaration

# Lesson 158                                    Unit 24

Finish learning your vocabulary unit. Read each word and its definition. Use the space below each word to write a synonym, write a sentence containing the word, draw a picture, or use some other device to help you commit the definitions to memory. You will have a quiz in Lesson 160.

- **realistic** (adj) aware or expressing awareness of things as they really are; not abstract

- **ruse** (n) a deceptive maneuver, especially to avoid capture

- **submerge** (v) sink below the surface; cover completely or make imperceptible

- **trait** (n) a distinguishing feature

- **venerable** (adj) impressive by reason of age; profoundly honored

- **zooty** (adj) flashy in manner or style

Unscramble your vocabulary words. Study for your vocabulary quiz tomorrow. Make sure you know your words. Study ideas: read them out loud, copy the ones you are unsure of, have someone quiz you, use the words in conversation.

S U E R _____
a deceptive maneuver, especially to avoid capture

R A I D N _____
an extreme state of adversity

I A T R T _____
a distinguishing feature

O T Y O Z _____
flashy in manner or style

M N A E D E _____
reduce in worth or character, usually verbally

L E P X E P R _____
be a mystery or bewildering to

T B R S S U T E _____
to make stronger or defensible

I I E N T M M N _____
close in time; about to occur

Y U Q I I T N I _____
morally objectionable behavior

(continued on the next page)

BOBLYSTI

_____

someone employed to persuade legislators to vote in a way that favors their employer

BMUERSEG

_____

sink below the surface

IVNETRGDE

_____

moving apart from a standard

ECREAEXLB

_____

of very poor quality or condition

URSIFOCTA

_____

stubbornly resistant to authority or control

NREPOOUPT

_____

suitable or at a time that is advantageous

RCIAELSIT

_____

aware or expressing awareness of things as they really are

NLERVEEAB

_____

impressive by reason of age

OTTINASANG

_____

someone who offers opposition

LEDCNCNEOO

_____

an expression of sympathy with another's grief

MGLPUAOTRE

_____

state or announce

You can study your words before you take this quiz, but you MUST put them away before you take the quiz. Cheaters get ZERO points for their quiz. Check your answers and record your score on your grade sheet.

Circle the letter that contains the word that *best* fits.

1.  The novel's _____ was the protagonist's brother.

    a. buttress       b. lobbyist       c. antagonist       d. nadir

2.  The coach was known to _____ his players when they were losing a game.

    a. demean       b. submerge       c. perplex       d. promulgate

3.  The celebrity's _____ outfit drew the media's attention.

    a. realistic       b. imminent       c. zooty       d. divergent

4.  She can tell a storm is _____ due to the aches in her bones.

    a. execrable       b. fractious       c. venerable       d. imminent

5.  A synonym for *bewilder*.

    a. promulgate       b. submerge       c. buttress       d. perplex

Fill in the blank with the word that *best* fits.

6.  An expression of sympathy with another's grief: _____.

7.  Someone who is stubbornly resistant to authority is _____.

8.  An extreme state of adversity is _____.

9.  A distinguishing feature is known as a(n) _____.

10. To state or announce is to _____.

# Lesson 161          Units 22-24 Review

Look over all of your words and notes from Units 22-24. Go over any rough spots in your memory.

# Lesson 162          Units 22-24 Review

Find a partner to help you with this review game. See if you can guess the vocabulary word in ten guesses or less. Guess letters one at a time for each word and have your partner fill them in or let you know they're not in the word.

— — — — — — — — — —        — — — — — — —
Hint: consider hallowed            Hint: countless

— — — — — — —        — — — — — — — —
Hint: clear and bright            Hint: polish

— — — — — — — — —        — — — — —
Hint: pronounce not guilty            Hint: lowest point

— — — — — — — — —        — — — — — — —
Hint: short account of an incident        Hint: lacking foresight

— — — — — — — — —        — — — — —
Hint: unjust act            Hint: distinguishing feature

# Lesson 163

Match the word to its definition.

1. deleterious      _____ a deceptive maneuver

2. licentious      _____ moving apart from a standard

3. inimical      _____ lacking moral discipline

4. prolific      _____ grow and flourish

5. imminent      _____ harmful to living things

6. ruse      _____ slow and apathetic

7. tractable      _____ make senseless or dizzy

8. torpid      _____ about to occur

9. illicit      _____ great in size

10. dither      _____ continuing indefinitely

11. divergent      _____ easily managed

12. stupefy      _____ make more complicated

13. burgeon      _____ intellectually productive

14. immense      _____ flashy in manner or style

15. perplex      _____ act nervously

16. zooty      _____ not friendly

17. perpetual      _____ forbidden by law

# Lesson 164

Units 22-24 Review

Can you find all 60 of your vocabulary words in this massive word search? Flip back through your three units for the word list if you need it.

```
H Z L B A M N N O Y B Q R C O I L Y M D I S S I D E N T T S
O T I M M I N E N T Z E S T N N I L C O N D O L E N C E W U
I M M E N S E N A T U R G P E I C U L P P A K N Q S M S B B
O M R W T Z B H K X T C W Z X M E X I B E E J D E R U E L M
P K V A R I A B L E W D G R C I N I V L U R Q S F T W O H E
P D W Z D I V E R G E N T N U C T C Q E L T F E D P R P N R
O O T E M K U Q A I R S B Z L A I R O A N I T U Q Y M L A G
R D K P R O M U L G A T E W P L O Y Y N J E C R N B Y A D E
T Z E L E N Q V H R N T A T A F U X T G D B R I E C P J I L
U I X M O Z D O I N P R L G T M S F G B I I L A T S T T R E
N N P L E J O M A B Y A W Z E U R W X U C E T I B P S O T H
E I M V G A P N I N E I R E A L I S T I C N X I P L H R R G
Z Q N R L O N I N E O T E X A S P E R A T I O N O V E P L Y
W U L U N D W P H W Z N D H K T Z D D D X K A U G N R I M P
F I M S S E K O E E P I Y S V A R I E G A T E D Y S V D A B
L T Y E T L D T R P N G C M R E V E R E N C E B O R W V W L
O Y R K U E E E R I D A N O Q B R T Q D J B W M C N Y V V
R Z I B P T M N N O T Y I N L U P A A J J I U R I B A L D F
I O A U E E A T T L V D S N T R S R Q N F Z T V T L A K J O
D O D R F R G N F I T W L I U A U J O R C W E H K H B F D R
T T I N Y I O J R F R J L V M X G P G F F O J P E C N R C T
R Y P I I O G E P I I E G V Q D S O N P I S R G H R L A B U
A X E S H U U S V C C O N D I T I O N A L C H Z T Y P C U I
C Y R H A S E W V S K M Q N T K A P O I E J I T H L R T R T
T N P Y E X E C R A B L E M G O G P L M S M Y E E R Y I G O
A H E E J Q P J L O B B Y I S T C X I F W T S X N N D O E U
B S T R I N G E N T X H O Z A X Z Z M P E J F C A T V U O S
L A U M R I M A N T P J V M V C D E P K S M Y O P I C S N W
E R A N C O R O U S A K O B R K K O I R M Z P E R P L E X S
R Q L D N I M S V D A N E C D O T E D F C M L O G T S N N Z
```

# Lesson 165                    Units 22-24 Review Quiz

If you got 100% on all three of your vocabulary quizzes so far, no vocab for you today. Way to go! If you didn't, take this review quiz. If you score higher on this than you did on one of your previous quizzes, you may replace the grade of one of those quizzes on your grade sheet (just one).

Circle the letter that contains the word that *best* fits.

1. The _____ snowstorms kept us home for weeks.

    a. perfunctory      b. perpetual      c. ribald      d. opportune

2. My _____ rug adds life to the room.

    a. rancorous      b. perfunctory      c. variegated      d. stringent

3. The athlete lifted weights to _____ his body.

    a. condition      b. omit      c. demean      d. promulgate

4. You need to _____ the chicken in the broth to keep it from drying out.

    a. submerge      b. ribald      c. demagogue      d. zephyr

5. His teenager answered most questions with _____ nods.

    a. omnipotent      b. anonymous      c. perfunctory      d. florid

Fill in the blank with the word that *best* fits.

6. Vigorous and enthusiastic enjoyment is _____.

7. Something of very poor quality is _____.

8. Stubbornly resistant to authority or control is _____.

9. A synonym for *exclude* might be _____.

10. A feeling of great annoyance is known as _____.

# Lesson 166

Find a partner to help you with this review game. See if you can guess the vocabulary word in ten guesses or less. Guess letters one at a time for each word and have your partner fill them in or let you know they're not in the word.

— — — — — — — — — —
Hint: of great significance

— — — — — — — —
Hint: the second of two

— — — — — — — — — —
Hint: damage the reputation of

— — — — — — — — —
Hint: in an earliest state

— — — — — — — — — —
Hint: extremely silly

— — — — — — — — — —
Hint: friendly

— — — — — — — —
Hint: mire

— — — — — — — —
Hint: extremely wicked

— — — — — — —
Hint: characterized by dignity

— — — — — — — —
Hint: act in accordance with rules

— — — — — — — —
Hint: admonish

— — — — — — — —
Hint: ideally perfect state

Match the word to its definition.

1. coalesce      _____ concoct something artificial or untrue

2. hapless      _____ liveliness and eagerness

3. alacrity      _____ praise, glorify, or honor

4. solicitous      _____ insincerely emotional

5. puerile      _____ a difficult problem

6. mawkish      _____ displaying a lack of maturity

7. assimilate      _____ a perfect embodiment of a concept

8. fabricate      _____ weaken mentally or morally

9. cogent      _____ fuse together

10. vituperate      _____ make unclear

11. vitriolic      _____ spread negative information about

12. paragon      _____ become similar to one's environment

13. extol      _____ full of anxiety and concern

14. mendacious      _____ given to lying

15. enervate      _____ powerfully persuasive

16. obfuscate      _____ harsh or corrosive in tone

17. conundrum      _____ inciting pity

# Lesson 168

Can you find the listed words from Units 1-3 in this word search? Say the definition as you circle the word. If you can't, go back and look it up before moving on.

```
S  J  C  B  L  O  S  A  G  A  C  I  O  U  S  N  M  A  G  F  N  B  L  E  A
H  M  N  A  I  C  I  I  S  K  P  X  C  A  C  O  P  H  O  N  Y  O  S  N  N
F  P  F  A  L  P  G  N  M  C  X  T  A  V  H  B  K  Y  V  N  A  I  Z  B  P
R  R  Y  X  N  U  R  P  T  P  F  E  B  U  L  L  I  E  N  T  X  T  G  X  E
M  O  O  S  Z  T  M  O  E  R  E  Q  V  V  M  Y  P  Q  L  Z  A  O  O  V  R
V  S  Q  A  W  S  I  N  I  R  A  T  Z  P  V  F  E  C  K  X  G  B  P  X  S
E  A  S  Y  M  R  P  P  Y  J  T  N  U  K  E  R  R  X  O  K  C  J  Q  O  P
C  I  A  B  T  L  N  S  A  X  Q  I  S  O  I  T  L  I  P  S  A  F  C  N  I
A  C  Q  K  I  B  O  G  H  T  M  C  N  I  U  Z  U  V  P  E  W  Z  W  O  C
M  F  B  V  E  R  D  A  N  T  H  V  F  A  G  S  A  L  T  P  D  F  R  F  A
A  I  N  S  I  D  I  O  U  S  T  Y  C  I  C  E  Q  C  A  W  E  I  X  Y  C
R  P  B  P  Z  N  C  R  Y  S  H  R  H  J  D  I  N  V  W  N  T  R  T  M  I
A  K  B  R  V  S  O  F  E  A  U  D  A  P  Q  A  O  T  E  N  C  P  Y  E  T
D  M  U  O  J  A  N  U  Q  C  T  B  V  N  S  X  S  U  E  V  D  E  O  Z  Y
E  Q  C  P  N  Z  F  W  L  V  A  A  S  O  S  E  N  G  S  Y  F  S  T  U  S
R  E  Q  I  W  W  L  Z  E  O  N  L  R  T  Y  I  I  A  T  U  B  Q  J  I  E
I  X  Y  T  L  T  A  I  X  T  Q  C  C  R  A  X  E  I  S  W  V  T  N  D  B
E  U  U  I  W  Y  G  B  E  B  A  U  C  I  E  N  S  N  D  C  A  I  G  H  S
G  E  O  O  A  T  R  D  M  S  X  A  A  N  T  N  T  O  T  P  E  J  E  W  S
P  H  K  U  E  T  A  E  P  V  W  Z  K  C  E  R  I  I  B  O  G  N  R  J  O
M  Y  U  S  T  Z  T  M  L  O  Y  W  K  P  I  I  A  I  A  D  T  Q  T  C  I
L  X  A  T  M  A  I  U  A  P  V  A  O  J  D  O  H  N  K  T  X  M  X  J  S
Z  Q  E  W  T  T  O  R  R  Y  N  R  Y  G  J  Y  U  E  T  N  E  N  C  E  M
D  R  T  A  N  O  N  E  Y  G  P  Y  E  H  U  G  M  S  Y  U  I  I  S  K  W
K  Y  V  E  R  A  C  I  T  Y  R  E  Y  V  I  M  P  E  R  V  I  O  U  S  C
```

| | | | | |
|---|---|---|---|---|
| antipathy | ebullient | impetuous | pertinacious | sacrosanct |
| cacophony | exemplary | insidious | petulance | sagacious |
| calumny | exigent | intransigent | propensity | substantiate |
| camaraderie | expedite | loquacious | propitious | transient |
| conflagration | frippery | nascent | prosaic | veracity |
| demure | impervious | perspicacity | recalcitrant | verdant |

# Lesson 169

Fill in the crossword puzzle with words from Units 13-15.

**Across:**
1. remote in manner
3. happen to
6. an empty area or space
8. failing to keep in mind
10. originating where it is found
12. never done or known before
13. express strong disapproval of
14. tendency to believe readily
15. extreme stinginess

**Down**:
2. a relaxed, comfortable feeling
4. make easier
5. someone who fights
7. a small or moderate amount
9. strong and sharp
11. lasting a very short time

Unscramble your vocabulary words.

**C A E N M U**
shrewdness shown by keen insight

_____

**I A L T D N U O A**
exaggerated and hypocritical praise

_____

**E A R T P E D E C**
belittle; express strong disapproval of

_____

**P I E X T E A**
make amends for

_____

**E E N P Y O H T**
a new participant in some activity; someone young or inexperienced

_____

**A N T C E H N T R**
clearly or sharply defined to the mind

_____

**A T G O A R R E**
assert one's right to

_____

**L P C A E I M L A B**
incapable of being appeased

_____

**L C N A N H O N T A**
marked by blithe unconcern

_____

(continued on the next page)

**SSNOEBTIEL**

appearing as such but not necessarily so; pretended

_____

**TYPIH**

concise and full of meaning

_____

**CCOSUR**

help in a difficult situation

_____

**RESTDCAEE**

violate the sacred character of a place or language

_____

**NEGUXPE**

remove by erasing or crossing out or as if by drawing a line

_____

**LPTUTDAEI**

a trite or obvious remark

_____

**TTCUNELUR**

defiantly aggressive

_____

**ERCIOBRPS**

command against

_____

**RTYROEDAGO**

expressive of low opinion

_____

**IEURN**

cause to accept or become hardened to; habituate

_____

**ENIGSNUA**

confidently optimistic and cheerful

_____

# Answers

## Lesson 4 — Unit 1 Practice

Fill in the crossword puzzle with your vocabulary words. Study for your vocabulary quiz tomorrow. Make sure you know your words. Study ideas: read them out loud, copy the ones you are unsure of, have someone quiz you, use the words in conversation.

Crossword answers (grid): PERSPICACITY, NASCENT, INSIDIOUS, SACROSANCT, CONFLAGRATION, TRANSIENT, FRAUDULENT, EXEMPLARY, SUBMISSIVE (with down words: DEMEASNOR/IMPROVE/etc.)

**Across:**
3. intelligence manifested by being astute
5. beginning
6. intended to entrap
8. must be kept sacred
13. a very intense and uncontrolled fire
15. one who stays only a short time
16. intended to deceive
18. worthy of imitation
19. willing to submit to orders or wishes of others

**Down:**
1. the way a person behaves toward others
2. not easily aroused or excited
3. a disposition to behave a certain way
4. loud, confusing, disagreeable sounds
7. turn aside
9. be against
10. unwillingness to tell lies
11. act in opposition to
12. duration of service
14. shorten
17. the state of being actual or real

## Lesson 5 — Unit 1 Quiz

You can study your words before you take this quiz, but you MUST put them away before you take the quiz. Cheaters get ZERO points for their quiz. Check your answers and record your score on your grade sheet (which can be printed online or found in the Language Arts workbook).

Circle the letter that contains the word that *best* fits.

1. The _____ of animal noises gave me a headache.
   **(a.) cacophony**   b. longevity   c. demeanor   d. veracity

2. His _____ behavior earned him the respect of the squad.
   a. fraudulent   b. insidious   **(c.) exemplary**   d. sacrosanct

3. The trench was dug to _____ the water away from the house.
   a. antagonize   b. oppose   c. abbreviate   **(d.) divert**

4. We had to _____ our lesson due to so many interruptions.
   a. oppose   **(b.) abbreviate**   c. antagonize   d. nascent

5. A synonym for inferno.
   a. transient   **(b.) conflagration**   c. demeanor   d. reality

Fill in the blank with the word that *best* fits.

6. The state of being actual or real is known as _____ **reality** _____.

7. Something intended to deceive is _____ **fraudulent** _____.

8. An unwillingness to tell lies is _____ **veracity** _____.

9. Someone's _____ **demeanor** _____ is the way they behave toward others.

10. A disposition to behave a certain way is a _____ **propensity** _____.

## Lesson 9 — Unit 2 Practice

Find your vocabulary words in the word search. As you find each one, repeat its definition. Look it up if you can't remember it. Study for your vocabulary quiz tomorrow. Make sure you know your words. Study ideas: read them out loud, copy the ones you are unsure of, have someone quiz you, use the words in conversation.

| | | | |
|---|---|---|---|
| abstract | docile | loquacious | rebuke |
| anticipate | exigent | nautical | sagacious |
| calumny | frippery | opulent | subordinate |
| conformist | impervious | pertinacious | translucent |
| demure | integrity | propitious | verdant |

## Lesson 10 — Unit 2 Quiz

You can study your words before you take this quiz, but you MUST put them away before you take the quiz. Cheaters get ZERO points for their quiz. Check your answers and record your score on your grade sheet.

Circle the letter that contains the word that *best* fits.

1. Sometimes quiet people become quite _____ when they're nervous.
   a. nautical   **(b.) loquacious**   c. abstract   d. translucent

2. The _____ businessman closed the deal.
   **(a.) sagacious**   b. verdant   c. abstract   d. exigent

3. Skipping the _____, the couple bought a new home instead of having a showy wedding.
   a. calumny   b. integrity   **(c.) frippery**   d. rebuke

4. He loves to read under the _____ pines.
   **(a.) verdant**   b. conformist   c. impervious   d. nautical

5. A synonym for shy.
   a. docile   b. rebuke   **(c.) demure**   d. integrity

Fill in the blank with the word that *best* fits.

6. Something that exists only in the mind is known as _____ **abstract** _____.

7. Someone who adheres to established standards of conduct is a _____ **conformist** _____.

8. Something that is _____ **translucent** _____ allows light to pass through diffusely.

9. Ostentatiously rich and superior in quality: _____ **opulent** _____.

10. An expression of criticism is a _____ **rebuke** _____.

## Lesson 14 — Unit 3 Practice

Unscramble your vocabulary words. Study for your vocabulary quiz tomorrow. Make sure you know your words. Study ideas: read them out loud, copy the ones you are unsure of, have someone quiz you, use the words in conversation.

FSEU _____ **fuse**
an electrical device that can interrupt the flow of current when overloaded

GAIAYTSC _____ **sagacity**
the trait of forming opinions by distinguishing and evaluating

STEUASTAINTB _____ **substantiate**
establish or strengthen as with new evidence or facts

TLELINEUB _____ **ebullient**
joyously unrestrained

DRAMCEIAEAR _____ **camaraderie**
the quality of affording easy familiarity and sociability

ROAOTR _____ **orator**
a person who delivers a speech

NLNIGTGEE _____ **negligent**
characterized by neglect and undue lack of concern

MPOUUSIET _____ **impetuous**
marked by violent force

SNRTATUME _____ **transmute**
change in outward structure or looks; alter the nature of (elements)

(continued on the next page)

## Lesson 14 — Unit 3 Practice (cont.)

TIRCENTRLACA _____ **recalcitrant**
stubbornly resistant to authority or control

COISPAR _____ **prosaic**
not fanciful or imaginative; lacking wit

GTNNTAIIERSN _____ **intransigent**
impervious to pleas, persuasion, requests, reason

CTEDIP _____ **depict**
show in a picture; give a description of; make a portrait of

EXV _____ **vex**
cause annoyance in; disturb

ANGNOOIRGECT _____ **congregation**
an assemblage of people or things collected together

EIPDEEXT _____ **expedite**
speed up the progress of; process fast and efficiently

ACICERB _____ **acerbic**
sour or bitter in taste; harsh or corrosive in tone

PTAATNHYI _____ **antipathy**
a feeling of intense dislike

AVIRLTECU _____ **lucrative**
producing a sizeable profit

EUTPCNLEA _____ **petulance**
an irritable feeling

## Lesson 15 — Unit 3 Quiz

You can study your words before you take this quiz, but you MUST put them away before you take the quiz. Cheaters get ZERO points for their quiz. Check your answers and record your score on your grade sheet.

Circle the letter that contains the word that *best* fits.

1. The _____ between a boy and his dog is unparalleled.
   a. congregation   b. fuse   c. orator   **(d.) camaraderie**

2. Our _____ lives have made us forget how to appreciate art.
   **(a.) prosaic**   b. recalcitrant   c. intransigent   d. lucrative

3. The _____ delivered the speech with professionalism.
   a. sagacity   **(b.) orator**   c. antipathy   d. petulance

4. The _____ song made her dance in her chair.
   a. acerbic   b. intransigent   c. recalcitrant   **(d.) ebullient**

5. A synonym for annoy.
   **(a.) vex**   b. transmute   c. depict   d. expedite

Fill in the blank with the word that *best* fits.

6. A synonym for sour: __**acerbic**__.

7. To show in picture is to __**depict**__.

8. Being characterized by undue haste and lack of thought is being __**impetuous**__.

9. A feeling of intense dislike is __**antipathy**__.

10. Something producing a sizeable profit is __**lucrative**__.

## Lesson 17 — Units 1-3 Review

Find a partner to help you with this review game. See if you can guess the vocabulary word in ten guesses or less. Guess letters one at a time for each word and have your partner fill them in or let you know they're not in the word.

e x e m p l a r y
Hint: worthy of imitation

d e m u r e
Hint: shy

d o c i l e
Hint: easily handled

p r o s a i c
Hint: lacking wit

e b u l l i e n t
Hint: joyously unrestrained

d i v e r t
Hint: turn aside

v e r a c i t y
Hint: unwillingness to lie

r e b u k e
Hint: censure severely

e x p e d i t e
Hint: speed up the process

f u s e
Hint: mix together

## Lesson 18 — Units 1-3 Review

Match the word to its definition.

1. abbreviate — __4__ a feeling of intense dislike
2. nascent — __12__ demanding attention
3. sagacious — __14__ must be kept sacred
4. antipathy — __5__ false accusation of an offense
5. calumny — __17__ ostentatiously rich and superior in quality
6. sagacity — __8__ full of trivial conversation
7. intransigent — __16__ beguiling but harmful
8. loquacious — __1__ shorten
9. verdant — __10__ sour or bitter in taste
10. acerbic — __3__ acutely insightful and wise
11. substantiate — __15__ one who stays only a short time
12. exigent — __2__ beginning
13. perspicacity — __13__ intelligence manifested by being astute
14. sacrosanct — __7__ impervious to requests and reason
15. transient — __11__ strengthen with new evidence
16. insidious — __6__ ability to understand and discriminate between relations
17. opulent — __9__ characterized by an abundance of lush green vegetation

## Lesson 19 — Units 1-3 Review

Can you find all 60 of your vocabulary words in this massive word search? Flip back through your three units for the word list if you need it.

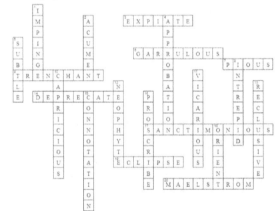

## Lesson 20 — Units 1-3 Review Quiz

If you got 100% on all three of your vocabulary quizzes so far, no vocab for you today. Way to go! If you didn't, take this review quiz. If you score higher on this than you did on one of your previous quizzes, you may replace the grade of one of those quizzes on your grade sheet (just one).

Circle the letter that contains the word that *best* fits.

1. Don't _____ your sister, get along!

   a. anticipate   **b. antagonize**   c. depict   d. transmute

2. The clerk wouldn't cash the _____ check.

   a. impassive   b. pertinacious   c. recalcitrant   **d. fraudulent**

3. A synonym for annoy.

   a. transmute   **b. vex**   c. anticipate   d. oppose

4. An antonym of concrete.

   **a. abstract**   b. impassive   c. submissive   d. propitious

5. The _____ teenager gets into trouble often.

   a. lucrative   b. nautical   **c. recalcitrant**   d. impassive

Fill in the blank with the word that *best* fits.

6. Something relating to ships or navigation is known as __**nautical**__.

7. Not capable of being affected by something is being __**impervious**__.

8. An inclination to do something is a __**propensity**__.

9. Stubbornly unyielding: __**pertinacious**__.

10. To be characterized by neglect and undue lack of concern is to be __**negligent**__.

## Lesson 24 — Unit 4 Practice

Fill in the crossword puzzle with your vocabulary words. Study for your vocabulary quiz tomorrow. Make sure you know your words. Study ideas: read them out loud, copy the ones you are unsure of, have someone quiz you, use the words in conversation.

**Across:**
3. make amends for
6. full of trivial conversation
7. showing reverence for a deity
9. clearly or sharply defined to the mind
14. express strong disapproval of
17. excessively or hypocritically pious
19. be greater in significance than
20. a powerful circular current of water

**Down:**
1. infringe upon
2. shrewdness shown by keen insight
4. official approval
5. difficult to detect or grasp
8. invulnerable to fear or intimidation
10. changeable
11. experienced at secondhand
12. someone young or inexperienced
13. withdrawn from society
15. an idea that is implied or suggested
16. command against
18. point

## Lesson 25 — Unit 4 Quiz

You can study your words before you take this quiz, but you MUST put them away before you take the quiz. Cheaters get ZERO points for their quiz. Check your answers and record your score on your grade sheet.

Circle the letter that contains the word that *best* fits.

1. Her business _____ was unparalleled.
   - a. connotation
   - b. eclipse
   - **c. acumen** (circled)
   - d. maelstrom

2. We couldn't believe it when our _____ friend auditioned for the musical.
   - **a. reclusive** (circled)
   - b. trenchant
   - c. vicarious
   - d. capricious

3. The powerful _____ brought down the ship.
   - a. eclipse
   - **b. maelstrom** (circled)
   - c. approbation
   - d. orient

4. His _____ attempt at humor was lost on me.
   - a. vicarious
   - b. reclusive
   - c. intrepid
   - **d. subtle** (circled)

5. To command against.
   - a. impinge
   - **b. proscribe** (circled)
   - c. expiate
   - d. deprecate

Fill in the blank with the word that *best* fits.

6. An official approval is an **approbation**.

7. To belittle is to **deprecate**.

8. When you advance beyond the usual limit, you **impinge**.

9. To determine your position relative to another point is to **orient**.

10. Experienced at secondhand: **vicarious**.

## Lesson 29 — Unit 5 Practice

Find your vocabulary words in the word search. As you find each one, repeat its definition. Look it up if you can't remember it. Study for your vocabulary quiz tomorrow. Make sure you know your words. Study ideas: read them out loud, copy the ones you are unsure of, have someone quiz you, use the words in conversation.

| | | |
|---|---|---|
| adhere | effrontery | malediction | reconciliation |
| arrogate | exploit | nonchalant | sanction |
| censure | generalize | ostensible | succor |
| consecutive | implacable | pithy | trilateral |
| derogatory | intuitive | prosperity | vicissitude |

## Lesson 30 — Unit 5 Quiz

You can study your words before you take this quiz, but you MUST put them away before you take the quiz. Cheaters get ZERO points for their quiz. Check your answers and record your score on your grade sheet.

Circle the letter that contains the word that *best* fits.

1. You need to strictly _____ to the rules to be a member at that club.
   - a. arrogate
   - b. generalize
   - c. exploit
   - **d. adhere** (circled)

2. The soldier was sent home after receiving another _____ from his superior officer.
   - a. effrontery
   - **b. censure** (circled)
   - c. malediction
   - d. prosperity

3. The Red Cross provided _____ after the hurricane.
   - a. reconciliation
   - b. vicissitude
   - c. censure
   - **d. succor** (circled)

4. The _____ book title told me all I needed to know.
   - **a. pithy** (circled)
   - b. consecutive
   - c. implacable
   - d. nonchalant

5. We received _____ to proceed with the plan.
   - a. prosperity
   - **b. sanction** (circled)
   - c. malediction
   - d. exploit

Fill in the blank with the word that *best* fits.

6. A curse: **malediction**.

7. A notable achievement: **exploit**.

8. Something that is **derogatory** is expressive of low opinion.

9. A three-sided polygon is a **trilateral**.

10. One after the other is known as **consecutive**.

## Lesson 34 — Unit 6 Practice

Unscramble your vocabulary words. Study for your vocabulary quiz tomorrow. Make sure you know your words. Study ideas: read them out loud, copy the ones you are unsure of, have someone quiz you, use the words in conversation.

ETRCDESAE     **desecrate**
violate the sacred character of a place or language

UTSONNTTICE     **constituent**
a citizen who is represented in a government by officials for whom he or she votes

LUITEDTPA     **platitude**
a trite or obvious remark

ECICSTA     **ascetic**
someone who practices self-denial as a spiritual discipline

ASHERCCRIATCIT     **characteristic**
typical or distinctive

CERITCEGNO     **egocentric**
a self-centered person with little regard for others

IVIYLF     **vilify**
spread negative information about

UNNEASIG     **sanguine**
confidently optimistic and cheerful

OTNLAUADI     **adulation**
exaggerated and hypocritical praise

(continued on the next page)

## Lesson 34 — Unit 6 Practice (cont.)

TAALOISNG      **nostalgia**
longing for something past

XUGENEP      **expunge**
remove by erasing or crossing out or as if by drawing a line

ETPNUDMI      **impudent**
marked by casual disrespect; improperly forward or bold

FLRIIPUESCA      **superficial**
concerned with or comprehending only what is apparent or obvious

RPOANTE      **protean**
taking on different forms

GIGNALR      **glaring**
looking at with a fixed glaze; shining intensely

ALEALMLEB      **malleable**
capable of being shaped or bent or drawn out

ETUCDRITE      **rectitude**
righteousness as a consequence of being honorable and honest

TUCLENTRU      **truculent**
defiantly aggressive

ITTNATOEUSOS      **ostentatious**
intended to attract notice and impress others

NEIRU      **inure**
cause to accept or become hardened to

## Lesson 35 — Unit 6 Quiz

You can study your words before you take this quiz, but you MUST put them away before you take the quiz. Cheaters get ZERO points for their quiz. Check your answers and record your score on your grade sheet.

Circle the letter that contains the word that *best* fits.

1. My brother was _____ at me when I used his computer without asking.
   - a. protean   b. ostentatious   c. impudent   **(d.) glaring**

2. Flying is _____ of flies.
   - a. ascetic   **(b.) characteristic**   c. truculent   d. malleable

3. The _____ girl had trouble making friends.
   - **(a.) egocentric**   b. inure   c. ostentatious   d. sanguine

4. Certain smells take me back to my childhood and make me feel strong _____.
   - a. rectitude   b. ascetic   **(c.) nostalgia**   d. adulation

5. A synonym for habituate.
   - **(a.) inure**   b. desecrate   c. expunge   d. glaring

Fill in the blank with the word that *best* fits.

6. Exaggerated and hypocritical praise is **adulation**.

7. Capable of being shaped is known as **malleable**.

8. Intended to attract notice and impress others: **ostentatious**.

9. Taking on different forms is known as **protean**.

10. A trite or obvious remark is a(n) **platitude**.

## Lesson 37 — Units 4-6 Review

Find a partner to help you with this review game. See if you can guess the vocabulary word in ten guesses or less. Guess letters one at a time for each word and have your partner fill them in or let you know they're not in the word.

**a d u l a t i o n**
Hint: exaggerated praise

**o r i e n t**
Hint: point

**a c u m e n**
Hint: keen insight

**e x p l o i t**
Hint: notable achievement

**d e s e c r a t e**
Hint: violate sacred character

**p i t h y**
Hint: full of meaning

**i n t r e p i d**
Hint: invulnerable to fear

**s u c c o r**
Hint: help during difficult times

**a r r o g a t e**
Hint: assert one's right to

**i n u r e**
Hint: habituate

## Lesson 38 — Units 4-6 Review

Match the word to its definition.

1. approbation — _4_ taking on different forms
2. ostensible — _7_ changeable
3. ascetic — _11_ a curse
4. protean — _9_ self-centered
5. derogatory — _13_ capable of being shaped or bent
6. garrulous — _2_ pretended
7. capricious — _17_ longing for something past
8. adhere — _10_ defiantly aggressive
9. egocentric — _1_ official approval
10. truculent — _15_ withdrawn from society
11. malediction — _5_ expressive of low opinion
12. impudent — _14_ incapable of being pleased
13. malleable — _8_ stick to firmly
14. implacable — _16_ give permission to
15. reclusive — _6_ full of trivial conversation
16. sanction — _12_ marked by casual disrespect
17. nostalgia — _3_ practicing great self-denial

## Lesson 39 — Units 4-6 Review

Can you find all 60 of your vocabulary words in this massive word search? Flip back through the three units for the word list if you need it.

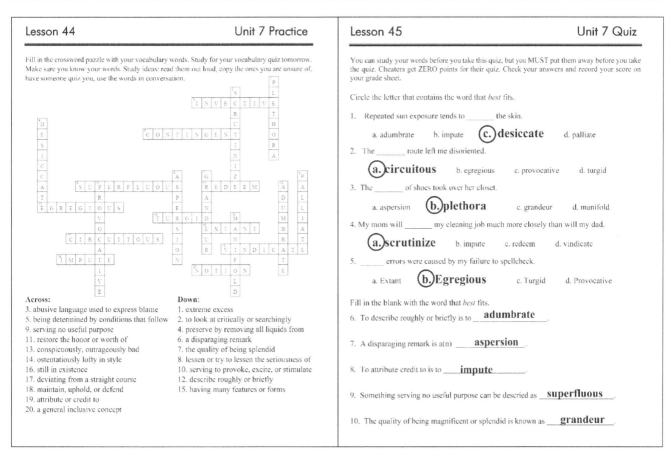

## Lesson 40 — Units 4-6 Review Quiz

If you got 100% on all three of your vocabulary quizzes so far, no vocab for you today. Way to go! If you didn't, take this review quiz. If you score higher on this than you did on one of your previous quizzes, you may replace the grade of one of those quizzes on your grade sheet (just one).

Circle the letter that contains the word that *best* fits.

1. The politician created an ad to _____ his opponent.
   a. generalize  **b. vilify**  c. expiate  d. adhere

2. The juror had the _____ to challenge the expert's opinion.
   **a. effrontery**  b. prosperity  c. constituent  d. connotation

3. You should not _____ your own worth.
   a. expiate  **b. deprecate**  c. generalize  d. expunge

4. The girl gave a _____ shrug.
   a. trilateral  b. sanctimonious  c. vicarious  **d. nonchalant**

5. The fur coat was a bit _____ for the funeral.
   a. intuitive  b. consecutive  **c. ostentatious**  d. trenchant

Fill in the blank with the word that *best* fits.

6. A new participant in an activity is a(n) ____ **neophyte** ____.

7. An idea that is implied or suggested is a(n) ____ **connotation** ____.

8. To be greater in significance than is to ____ **eclipse** ____.

9. To be excessively or hypocritically pious is to be ____ **sanctimonious** ____.

10. Something involving three parties is known as ____ **trilateral** ____.

## Lesson 44 — Unit 7 Practice

Fill in the crossword puzzle with your vocabulary words. Study for your vocabulary quiz tomorrow. Make sure you know your words. Study ideas: read them out loud, copy the ones you are unsure of, have someone quiz you, use the words in conversation.

**Across:**
3. abusive language used to express blame
5. being determined by conditions that follow
9. serving no useful purpose
11. restore the honor or worth of
13. conspicuously, outrageously bad
14. ostentatiously lofty in style
16. still in existence
17. deviating from a straight course
18. maintain, uphold, or defend
19. attribute or credit to
20. a general inclusive concept

**Down:**
1. extreme excess
2. to look at critically or searchingly
4. preserve by removing all liquids from
6. a disparaging remark
7. the quality of being splendid
8. lessen or try to lessen the seriousness of
10. serving to provoke, excite, or stimulate
12. describe roughly or briefly
15. having many features or forms

## Lesson 45 — Unit 7 Quiz

You can study your words before you take this quiz, but you MUST put them away before you take the quiz. Cheaters get ZERO points for their quiz. Check your answers and record your score on your grade sheet.

Circle the letter that contains the word that *best* fits.

1. Repeated sun exposure tends to _____ the skin.
   a. adumbrate  b. impute  **c. desiccate**  d. palliate

2. The _____ route left me disoriented.
   **a. circuitous**  b. egregious  c. provocative  d. turgid

3. The _____ of shoes took over her closet.
   a. aspersion  **b. plethora**  c. grandeur  d. manifold

4. My mom will _____ my cleaning job much more closely than will my dad.
   **a. scrutinize**  b. impute  c. redeem  d. vindicate

5. _____ errors were caused by my failure to spellcheck.
   a. Extant  **b. Egregious**  c. Turgid  d. Provocative

Fill in the blank with the word that *best* fits.

6. To describe roughly or briefly is to ____ **adumbrate** ____.

7. A disparaging remark is a(n) ____ **aspersion** ____.

8. To attribute credit to is to ____ **impute** ____.

9. Something serving no useful purpose can be described as ____ **superfluous** ____.

10. The quality of being magnificent or splendid is known as ____ **grandeur** ____.

## Lesson 49 — Unit 8 Practice

Find your vocabulary words in the word search. As you find each one, repeat its definition. Look it up if you can't remember it. Study for your vocabulary quiz tomorrow. Make sure you know your words. Study ideas: read them out loud, copy the ones you are unsure of, have someone quiz you, use the words in conversation.

```
A  S  X  S  M  D  T  N  O  V  I  C  E  H  Q  R  C  E  J  O
N  M  T  U  R  P  I  T  U  D  E  B  K  N  F  X  M  X  G  E
D  F  K  Z  G  R  P  V  P  R  I  Q  A  V  R  L  W  X  T  X
A  O  W  I  C  U  Z  D  F  V  D  D  E  Z  M  J  B  E  A  N
I  I  M  T  K  Q  I  H  Y  Q  N  S  Z  V  U  C  M  N  J
F  J  Q  T  E  L  Q  C  A  U  E  S  V  H  N  Y  O  P  D  A
P  V  M  M  L  X  N  K  D  X  A  Y  L  E  J  Z  P  R  I  G
K  Q  T  A  P  O  L  E  M  I  C  S  V  A  N  L  K  O  R  L
Z  B  P  H  U  M  R  Q  U  E  M  F  C  X  R  G  X  A  O  S
P  W  J  M  E  A  T  X  T  D  U  Y  X  G  A  O  P  I  N  Q  C
R  M  B  S  E  O  R  A  C  E  L  U  S  I  V  E  M  E  U  U
M  V  G  U  B  R  R  I  C  F  X  H  X  L  C  I  O  E  R
A  F  F  R  E  D  U  I  N  K  A  Y  S  D  N  T  U  N  R
X  K  D  F  N  C  R  V  D  O  D  I  Y  I  M  Q  V  S  E  L
X  Q  H  E  U  N  C  K  E  L  E  L  X  F  Y  U  F  E  L
V  B  V  I  P  Y  T  H  R  R  W  C  R  K  Z  L  N  F  O  U
J  N  Z  T  R  G  N  D  O  P  S  S  C  T  R  F  P  F  C  U
O  U  B  T  B  P  E  I  A  D  I  M  W  Q  I  T  C  I  O  S
G  F  B  T  G  O  H  I  F  R  T  X  T  N  I  I  V  J  A  O  A
L  O  F  W  L  O  W  A  X  M  Z  B  Y  M  Y  R  E  R  D  O
V  Q  T  C  O  N  T  R  A  D  I  C  T  I  O  Q  G  O  Y  X
```

| | | | |
|---|---|---|---|
| adversity | elusive | marauder | redundant |
| assert | extemporaneous | novice | scurrilous |
| circumvent | grandiloquence | pallid | surfeit |
| contradiction | inchoate | polemic | turpitude |
| devoid | inveterate | proximity | vindictive |

---

## Lesson 50 — Unit 8 Quiz

You can study your words before you take this quiz, but you MUST put them away before you take the quiz. Cheaters get ZERO points for their quiz. Check your answers and record your score on your grade sheet.

Circle the letter that contains the word that *best* fits.

1. Despite great _____, the team won the championship.
   a. grandiloquence   b. surfeit   **c.** **adversity**   d. turpitude

2. The _____ squirrel dropped acorns on my car when I forgot to refill the feeder.
   **a.** **vindictive**   b. redundant   c. pallid   d. extemporaneous

3. The speech was not supposed to be _____, but I forgot it was due today.
   a. pallid   **b.** **extemporaneous**   c. scurrilous   d. devoid

4. After laying on it all night, my arm was _____ of all feeling.
   a. elusive   **b.** **devoid**   c. inchoate   d. polemic

5. The article is a(n) _____ against those who are in power.
   **a.** **polemic**   b. adversity   c. marauder   d. surfeit

Fill in the blank with the word that *best* fits.

6. Opposition between two conflicting forces is known as ____**contradiction**____.

7. To state categorically is to ____**assert**____.

8. Something only partly in existence is ____**inchoate**____. inchoate

9. A synonym for *habitual*: ____**inveterate**____.

10. The state of being more than full is known as ____**surfeit**____.

---

## Lesson 54 — Unit 9 Practice

Unscramble your vocabulary words. Study for your vocabulary quiz tomorrow. Make sure you know your words. Study ideas: read them out loud, copy the ones you are unsure of, have someone quiz you, use the words in conversation.

YIVALNOTRAC ____**clairvoyant**____
perceiving things beyond the natural range of the senses

TIINLBCMAOEP ____**incompatible**____
not easy to combine harmoniously

CATVEAOD ____**advocate**____
a person who pleads for a cause

TNCROETI ____**contrite**____
feeling or expressing pain or sorrow for sins or offenses

PTNTEOR ____**portent**____
a sign of something about to happen

TENMEIN ____**eminent**____
standing above others in quality or position

DAMIUNL ____**maudlin**____
effusively or insincerely emotional

OIRGSRUGEA ____**gregarious**____
instinctively seeking and enjoying the company of others

IDUSUSOAS ____**assiduous**____
marked by care and persistent effort

(continued on the next page)

---

## Lesson 54 — Unit 9 Practice (cont.)

ACEPANA ____**panacea**____
hypothetical remedy for all ills or diseases

TENXEIUNGAT ____**extenuating**____
lessen or try to lessen the seriousness or extent of

UENCAN ____**nuance**____
a subtle difference in meaning or opinion or attitude

TBLNUAJI ____**jubilant**____
joyful and proud, especially because of triumph or success

USPAHDAINO ____**diaphanous**____
so thin as to transmit light

ERUTPND ____**prudent**____
careful and sensible

SMUIERS ____**surmise**____
infer from incomplete evidence

ESTDYIIENRP ____**serendipity**____
good luck in making unexpected and fortunate discoveries

RCLTEEF ____**reflect**____
manifest or bring back

TQIUOUUSIB ____**ubiquitous**____
being present everywhere at once

UCSVIOS ____**viscous**____
having a relatively high resistance to flow

## Lesson 55 — Unit 9 Quiz

You can study your words before you take this quiz, but you MUST put them away before you take the quiz. Cheaters get ZERO points for their quiz. Check your answers and record your score on your grade sheet.

Circle the letter that contains the word that *best* fits.

1. He was _____ in pointing out every detail.
   **(a.) assiduous**   b. diaphanous   c. gregarious   d. maudlin

2. She found it _____ to consult a financial advisor before investing.
   a. panacea   b. incompatible   **(c.) prudent**   d. clairvoyant

3. Cowboy hats are _____ in the country music scene.
   a. gregarious   b. viscous   **(c.) ubiquitous**   d. contrite

4. Cod liver oils is the time-honored _____.
   a. portent   **(b.) panacea**   c. surmise   d. nuance

5. A synonym for see-through.
   **(a.) diaphanous**   b. contrite   c. eminent   d. viscous

Fill in the blank with the word that *best* fits.

6. A subtle difference in meaning is known as __**nuance**__.

7. To infer from incomplete evidence is to __**surmise**__.

8. Being careful and sensible is being __**prudent**__.

9. To be joyful and proud is to be __**jubilant**__.

10. Something having a relatively high resistance to flow is __**viscous**__.

---

## Lesson 57 — Units 7-9 Review

Find a partner to help you with this review game. See if you can guess the vocabulary word in ten guesses or less. Guess letters one at a time for each word and have your partner fill them in or let you know they're not in the word.

a s p e r s i o n
Hint: a disparaging remark

n u a n c e
Hint: subtle difference

p a l l i d
Hint: dim or feeble

e l u s i v e
Hint: difficult to describe

a s s i d u o u s
Hint: marked by care

e x t a n t
Hint: not extinct

c o n t r i t e
Hint: expressing sorrow for sins

n o t i o n
Hint: a vague idea

a d v o c a t e
Hint: push for something

a s s e r t
Hint: declare as true

---

## Lesson 58 — Units 7-9 Review

Match the word to its definition.

1. adumbrate — _3_ partially excusing or justifying
2. inveterate — _5_ a corrupt act
3. extenuating — _9_ surround so as to force to give up
4. ubiquitous — _13_ of or involving dispute or controversy
5. turpitude — _1_ describe roughly or briefly
6. devoid — _15_ having a relatively high resistance to flow
7. desiccate — _11_ someone who attacks in search of booty
8. scrutinize — _16_ expressing offensive reproach
9. circumvent — _8_ look at critically or searchingly
10. gregarious — _17_ ostentatiously lofty in style
11. marauder — _14_ so thin as to transmit light
12. egregious — _4_ being present everywhere at once
13. polemic — _12_ outrageously bad
14. diaphanous — _2_ habitual
15. viscous — _6_ completely wanting or lacking
16. scurrilous — _10_ instinctively seeking and enjoying the company of others
17. turgid — _7_ lacking vitality or spirit

---

## Lesson 59 — Units 7-9 Review

Can you find all 60 of your vocabulary words in this massive word search? Flip back through the three units for the word list if you need it.

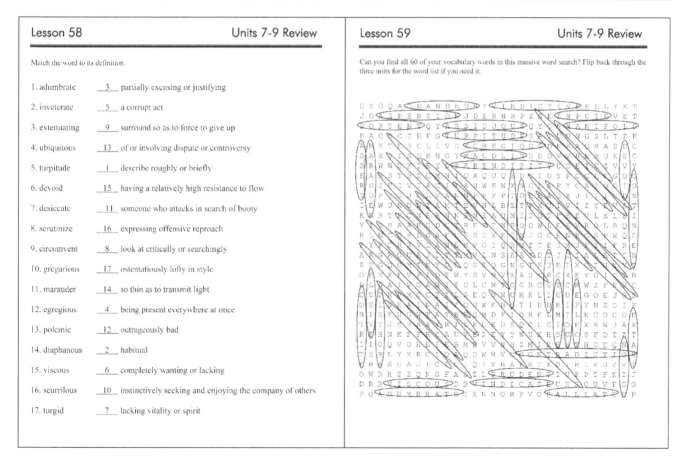

## Lesson 60 — Units 7-9 Review Quiz

If you got 100% on all three of your vocabulary quizzes so far, no vocab for you today. Way to go! If you didn't, take this review quiz. If you score higher on this than you did on one of your previous quizzes, you may replace the grade of one of those quizzes on your grade sheet (just one).

Circle the letter that contains the word that *best* fits.

1. Will the Florida _____ be joining the assembly?

    a. grandeur    b. invective    **(c.) contingent**    d. surfeit

2. The _____ display got us all in the Christmas spirit.

    **(a.) jubilant**    b. clairvoyant    c. redundant    d. circuitous

3. The aspirin served to _____ his pain.

    a. impute    **(b.) palliate**    c. surfeit    d. reflect

4. The drama queen behaved in a _____ way toward even the smallest incident.

    a. prudent    b. incompatible    **(c.) maudlin**    d. inchoate

5. The newspaper's _____ of the rally infuriated its organizers.

    **(a.) invective**    b. contingent    c. grandiloquence    d. panacea

Fill in the blank with the word that *best* fits.

6. Extreme excess: _____ **plethora** _____

7. Something serving to provoke or excite is known as _____ **provocative** _____ .

8. Something that serves no useful purpose is _____ **superfluous** _____ .

9. Something imperfectly formed is _____ **inchoate** _____ .

10. A sign of something about to happen is a _____ **portent** _____ .

---

## Lesson 64 — Unit 10 Practice

Fill in the crossword puzzle with your vocabulary words. Study for your vocabulary quiz tomorrow. Make sure you know your words. Study ideas: read them out loud, copy the ones you are unsure of, have someone quiz you, use the words in conversation.

Crossword answers: EMPATHY, SERVILE, UMBRAGE, CONUNDRUM, HACKNEYED, VITAL, PARAGON, INCONGRUOUS, MAWKISH, PRAGMATIC, EXTOL, REJUVENATE, SURREPTITIOUS

---

## Lesson 65 — Unit 10 Quiz

You can study your words before you take this quiz, but you MUST put them away before you take the quiz. Cheaters get ZERO points for their quiz. Check your answers and record your score on your grade sheet.

Circle the letter that contains the word that *best* fits.

1. I can't _____ to these cold winters!

    a. extol    b. rejuvenate    c. aesthetic    **(d.) assimilate**

2. Water and oil don't _____ .

    **(a.) coalesce**    b. obdurate    c. servile    d. prurient

3. The chef at Café Du Monde is a(n) _____ .

    a. conundrum    **(b.) paragon**    c. jubilation    d. umbrage

4. Our dog has _____ ways of sneaking table scraps.

    **(a.) surreptitious**    b. vital    c. incongruous    d. pragmatic

5. The weekend away will _____ your mind and body.

    a. extol    b. coalesce    **(c.) rejuvenate**    d. assimilate

Fill in the blank with the word that *best* fits.

6. Something repeated too often is _____ **hackneyed** _____ .

7. A synonym for *maudlin* might be _____ **mawkish** _____ .

8. A difficult problem is a(n) _____ **conundrum** _____ .

9. A feeling of anger caused by being offended is known as _____ **umbrage** _____ .

10. Something that's urgently needed is _____ **vital** _____ .

---

## Lesson 69 — Unit 11 Practice

Find your vocabulary words in the word search. As you find each one, repeat its definition. Look it up if you can't remember it. Study for your vocabulary quiz tomorrow. Make sure you know your words. Study ideas: read them out loud, copy the ones you are unsure of, have someone quiz you, use the words in conversation.

| | | | |
|---|---|---|---|
| affinity | empirical | mendacious | relegate |
| asylum | fabricate | obfuscate | skeptical |
| coalition | hapless | paramount | sustainable |
| convergence | inconsequential | precarious | uniform |
| differentiate | jumbled | puerile | vitriolic |

## Lesson 70 — Unit 11 Quiz

You can study your words before you take this quiz, but you MUST put them away before you take the quiz. Cheaters get ZERO points for their quiz. Check your answers and record your score on your grade sheet.

Circle the letter that contains the word that *best* fits.

1. Don't _____ a story, just tell me what happened to the lamp.

    a. differentiate    b. obfuscate    c. relegate    **(d.) fabricate**

2. The _____ of Jupiter and Saturn in the night sky was a sight to see.

    **(a.) convergence**    b. asylum    c. uniform    d. affinity

3. The _____ passengers were stranded at the airport during the winter storm.

    a. empirical    b. mendacious    **(c.) hapless**    d. paramount

4. My words become _____ when I get nervous.

    a. precarious    **(b.) jumbled**    c. vitriolic    d. sustainable

5. The _____ attack on the president was uncalled for.

    a. skeptical    **(b.) vitriolic**    c. empirical    d. precarious

Fill in the blank with the word that *best* fits.

6. A shelter from danger or hardship is _____ **asylum** .

7. To be given to lying is to be _____ **mendacious** .

8. When you make obscure or unclear, you _____ **obfuscate** .

9. Displaying or suggesting a lack of maturity is _____ **puerile** .

10. Having superior power or influence is being _____ **paramount** .

## Lesson 74 — Unit 12 Practice

Unscramble your vocabulary words. Study for your vocabulary quiz tomorrow. Make sure you know your words. Study ideas: read them out loud, copy the ones you are unsure of, have someone quiz you, use the words in conversation.

RTEAUPVTEI — _____ **vituperate**
spread negative information about

TRLECOAER — _____ **correlate**
mutually related

POYAHCSTN — _____ **sycophant**
a person who tries to please in order to gain personal advantage

SIEPORTCPUI — _____ **precipitous**
extremely steep

OVIIBRLRECTNETNO — _____ **incontrovertible**
impossible to deny

CARATLYI — _____ **alacrity**
liveliness and eagerness

BOELUIQ — _____ **oblique**
slanting

TUSFCAIOE — _____ **facetious**
cleverly amusing in tone

OSICUIOLST — _____ **solicitous**
full of anxiety and concern

(continued on the next page)

## Lesson 74 — Unit 12 Practice (cont.)

DEPCARH — _____ **parched**
extremely thirsty

EMNGTAU — _____ **augment**
enlarge or increase

IUSNPGCOUA — _____ **pugnacious**
tough by virtue of experience

ITIFDENDF — _____ **diffident**
showing modest reserve

GNRUHAEA — _____ **harangue**
address forcefully

OETNGC — _____ **cogent**
powerfully persuasive

VNREEATE — _____ **enervate**
weaken mentally or morally

RCRAMLEUI — _____ **mercurial**
liable to sudden, unpredictable change

OTRDSIJCIIUN — _____ **jurisdiction**
the territory within which power can be exercised

TLINUEAALR — _____ **unilateral**
involving only one part or side

TELRANEV — _____ **relevant**
having a bearing on or connection with the subject at issue

## Lesson 75 — Unit 12 Quiz

You can study your words before you take this quiz, but you MUST put them away before you take the quiz. Cheaters get ZERO points for their quiz. Check your answers and record your score on your grade sheet.

Circle the letter that contains the word that *best* fits.

1. The _____ climb up the mountain left us all exhausted and thirsty.

    a. relevant    b. incontrovertible    **(c.) precipitous**    d. facetious

2. The doctor's _____ statement convinced me to get the surgery.

    a. diffident    **(b.) cogent**    c. mercurial    d. unilateral

3. After a day of yard work in the sun, he was _____.

    **(a.) parched**    b. oblique    c. facetious    d. relevant

4. You can _____ your learning with various online options.

    a. harangue    b. vituperate    **(c.) augment**    d. correlate

5. A synonym for *misleading*.

    a. pugnacious    **(b.) oblique**    c. mercurial    d. solicitous

Fill in the blank with the word that *best* fits.

6. To be lacking self-confidence is to be _____ **diffident** .

7. To address forcefully is to _____ **harangue** .

8. A person who tries to please someone for personal gain is a(n) _____ **sycophant** .

9. Liveliness and eagerness is _____ **alacrity** .

10. Something involving only one part or side is _____ **unilateral** .

Find a partner to help you with this review game. See if you can guess the vocabulary word in ten guesses or less. Guess letters one at a time for each word and have your partner fill them in or let you know they're not in the word.

o  b  f  u  s  c  a  t  e
Hint: make unclear

c  o  g  e  n  t
Hint: powerfully persuasive

a  s  y  l  u  m
Hint: a shelter from danger

m  a  w  k  i  s  h
Hint: insincerely emotional

m  e  r  c  u  r  i  a  l
Hint: liable to sudden, unpredictable change

v  i  t  a  l
Hint: full of spirit

c  o  a  l  e  s  c  e
Hint: cause to grow together

e  x  t  o  l
Hint: praise, glorify

a  f  f  i  n  i  t  y
Hint: natural attraction

h  a  p  l  e  s  s
Hint: inciting pity

Match the word to its definition.

1. obdurate        __3__  liveliness and eagerness

2. empirical       __7__  a feeling of anger caused by being offended

3. alacrity        __12__ marked by quiet, caution, and secrecy

4. vituperate      __2__  derived from experiment or observation rather than theory

5. puerile         __14__ a difficult problem

6. servile         __9__  harsh or corrosive in tone

7. umbrage         __13__ given to lying

8. precarious      __5__  displaying a lack of maturity

9. vitriolic       __16__ weaken mentally or morally

10. oblique        __1__  stubbornly persistent in wrongdoing

11. convergence    __15__ repeated too often

12. surreptitious  __6__  submissive in attitude or behavior

13. mendacious     __10__ misleading

14. conundrum      __4__  spread negative information about

15. hackneyed      __17__ address forcefully

16. enervate       __11__ the occurrence of two or more things coming together

17. harangue       __8__  fraught with danger

Can you find all 60 of your vocabulary words in this massive word search? Flip back through the three units for the word list if you need it.

If you got 100% on all three of your vocabulary quizzes so far, no vocab for you today. Way to go! If you didn't, take this review quiz. If you score higher on this than you did on one of your previous quizzes, you may replace the grade of one of those quizzes on your grade sheet (just one).

Circle the letter that contains the word that *best* fits.

1. The scientist had a _____ approach to dealing with the water shortage.
   **a. pragmatic**    b. prurient    c. facetious    d. correlate

2. The _____ inquiry about my health was appreciated.
   a. unilateral    b. skeptical    **c. solicitous**    d. incongruous

3. The _____ of business owners sponsored a scholarship.
   a. differential    **b. coalition**    c. jurisdiction    d. sycophant

4. Playing in the basketball game left me _____.
   **a. parched**    b. precipitous    c. relevant    d. incongruous

5. The _____ mess of a room took hours to clean.
   a. pugnacious    b. incontrovertible    c. sustainable    **d. jumbled**

Fill in the blank with the word that *best* fits.

6. A synonym for law could be ____**jurisdiction**____.

7. Something that's capable of being maintained at a certain level is ____**sustainable**____.

8. To give new life or energy is to ____**rejuvenate**____.

9. To become similar to one's environment is to ____**assimilate**____.

10. A perfect embodiment of a concept is a ____**paragon**____.

## Lesson 84 — Unit 13 Practice

Fill in the crossword puzzle with your vocabulary words. Study for your vocabulary quiz tomorrow. Make sure you know your words. Study ideas: read them out loud, copy the ones you are unsure of, have someone quiz you, use the words in conversation.

Crossword answers:
PARIAH, DIFFUSE, METICULOUS, ALOOF, ENHANCE, VOID, CREDULITY, AUTHENTIC, PRECLUDE, COHESIVE, ENHANCE

## Lesson 85 — Unit 13 Quiz

You can study your words before you take this quiz, but you MUST put them away before you take the quiz. Cheaters get ZERO points for their quiz. Check your answers and record your score on your grade sheet.

Circle the letter that contains the word that *best* fits.

1. The new ramp will _____ the entry of wheelchairs into the building.
   a. diffuse    b. preclude    **c. facilitate**    d. relinquish

2. The beautiful flowers were at the height of their _____.
   a. pariah    **b. pulchritude**    c. void    d. credulity

3. A synonym for *increase*.
   **a. enhance**    b. diffuse    c. preclude    d. relinquish

4. Her _____ planning saved the day when the rain threatened to ruin the party.
   a. oblivious    b. aloof    **c. meticulous**    d. authentic

5. The injury will _____ him from an athletic career.
   **a. preclude**    b. diffuse    c. enhance    d. facilitate

Fill in the blank with the word that *best* fits.

6. Remote in manner is ____aloof____.

7. Sticking or holding together and resisting separation is being ____cohesive____.

8. A tendency to believe readily is ____credulity____.

9. A union of interests or purposes is known as ____solidarity____.

10. A person who is rejected from society or home is a ____pariah____.

## Lesson 89 — Unit 14 Practice

Find your vocabulary words in the word search. As you find each one, repeat its definition. Look it up if you can't remember it. Study for your vocabulary quiz tomorrow. Make sure you know your words. Study ideas: read them out loud, copy the ones you are unsure of, have someone quiz you, use the words in conversation.

| | | | |
|---|---|---|---|
| alternative | ephemeral | mishap | renovate |
| befall | fallacious | obscure | solipsistic |
| collaborate | haughty | parsimony | taciturn |
| criterion | indigenous | precocious | unprecedented |
| digression | justify | punctilious | wanton |

## Lesson 90 — Unit 14 Quiz

You can study your words before you take this quiz, but you MUST put them away before you take the quiz. Cheaters get ZERO points for their quiz. Check your answers and record your score on your grade sheet.

Circle the letter that contains the word that *best* fits.

1. The _____ with my computer cost me 10 hours of work.
   a. alternative    b. criterion    c. wanton    **d. mishap**

2. The _____ kindergartener won the K-5 spelling bee.
   a. obscure    **b. precocious**    c. fallacious    d. solipsistic

3. The neighbors decided to _____ to relocate the pesky chipmunk.
   **a. collaborate**    b. befall    c. obscure    d. justify

4. We will _____ the kitchen to get it the way we want it.
   a. wanton    **b. renovate**    c. ephemeral    d. indigenous

5. It was a giant _____ when we ended up discussing math in Spanish class.
   a. criterion    b. fallacious    **c. digression**    d. unprecedented

Fill in the blank with the word that *best* fits.

6. Believing that only the self exists is ____solipsistic____.

7. Marked by precise accordance with details is ____punctilious____.

8. Extreme stinginess is ____parsimony____.

9. Something lasting a very short time is ____ephemeral____.

10. Something that has never been done or known before is ____unprecedented____.

Unscramble your vocabulary words. Study for your vocabulary quiz tomorrow. Make sure you know your words. Study ideas: read them out loud, copy the ones you are unsure of, have someone quiz you, use the words in conversation.

A Y R W                                        _____ **wary** _____
marked by keen caution and watchful prudence

A T O S H P                                    _____ **pathos** _____
a quality that arouses emotions, especially pity or sorrow

R G N U L O A                                  _____ **languor** _____
a relaxed comfortable feeling

C U D M M O I                                  _____ **modicum** _____
a small or moderate amount

G E N P N T U                                  _____ **pungent** _____
strong and sharp

L A T U T F C                                  _____ **tactful** _____
having or showing a sense of what is fitting and considerate

R C T C I L I A                                _____ **critical** _____
marked by a tendency to find and call attention to errors and flaws

D N L E T I I G                                _____ **diligent** _____
quietly and steadily persevering, especially in detail or exactness

I D S T O H E N                                _____ **hedonist** _____
someone motivated by desires for sensual pleasures

(continued on the next page)

---

O L U S I O T N                                _____ **solution** _____
a statement that solves a problem

A B I O G U U S M                              _____ **ambiguous** _____
open to interpretation

Q B L E I A U T E                              _____ **equitable** _____
fair to all parties as dictated by reason or conscience

I P E R N T S C E                             _____ **prescient** _____
perceiving the significance of events before they occur

T R E O E P A R B                             _____ **reprobate** _____
deviating from what is considered moral or right

O M A N P C O S I S                           _____ **compassion** _____
a deep awareness of and sympathy for another's suffering

S T U S O I A I D F                           _____ **fastidious** _____
giving careful attention to detail

Q S S I U O O U B E                           _____ **obsequious** _____
attempting to win favor from influential people by flattery

Z I A E U R L N E D                           _____ **unrealized** _____
marked by failure to realize full potentialities

B L N R E I E L E G T                         _____ **belligerent** _____
someone who fights

D S T A N I R M E I I I N C                    _____ **indiscriminate** _____
failing to make or recognize distinctions

---

You can study your words before you take this quiz, but you MUST put them away before you take the quiz. Cheaters get ZERO points for their quiz. Check your answers and record your score on your grade sheet.

Circle the letter that contains the word that *best* fits.

1.  The _____ child was constantly in time out.

    a. ambiguous    **b. belligerent**    c. fastidious    d. obsequious

2.  The _____ nature of the instructions made them difficult to follow.

    a. pungent    b. prescient    **c. ambiguous**    d. wary

3.  We felt a _____ of relief with the test over, though the results were still to come.

    **a. modicum**    b. pathos    c. solution    d. hedonist

4.  My disorderly ways were quickly nipped in the bud by my _____ roommate.

    **a. fastidious**    b. equitable    c. reprobate    d. unrealized

5.  I fondly remember the _____ of sunny days at the lake.

    a. belligerent    b. compassion    c. modicum    **d. languor**

Fill in the blank with the word that *best* fits.

6.  A quality that arouses pity or sorrow is _____ **pathos** _____.

7.  Something deviating from what is considered moral or right is _____ **reprobate** _____.

8.  To be marked by keen caution and watchful prudence is to be _____ **wary** _____.

9.  To show sensitivity in dealing with people is to be _____ **tactful** _____.

10. A deep awareness of and sympathy for another's suffering is _____ **compassion** _____.

---

Find a partner to help you with this review game. See if you can guess the vocabulary word in ten guesses or less. Guess letters one at a time for each word and have your partner fill them in or let you know they're not in the word.

c r e d u l i t y
Hint: tendency to believe readily

b e f a l l
Hint: happen to

p a t h o s
Hint: a quality that arouses pity

p u n g e n t
Hint: strong and sharp

p a r s i m o n y
Hint: extreme stinginess

t a c i t
Hint: implied from actions

c o h e s i v e
Hint: well-integrated

m i s h a p
Hint: unfortunate, unpredictable outcome

h e d o n i s t
Hint: someone motivated by sensual desires

w a n t o n
Hint: spend wastefully

## Lesson 98           Units 13-15 Review

Match the word to its definition.

1. aloof      __3__ showing a sense of what is fitting and considerate

2. digression      __7__ increase

3. tactful      __10__ lasting a very short time

4. languor      __4__ a relaxed, comfortable feeling

5. reprobate      __12__ a small or moderate amount

6. pungent      __9__ physical beauty

7. enhance      __14__ marked by precise accordance with details

8. obscure      __1__ remote in manner

9. pulchritude      __15__ characteristic of exceptionally early development

10. ephemeral      __8__ make less visible or unclear

11. indiscriminate      __16__ open to interpretation

12. modicum      __5__ a person without moral scruples

13. indigenous      __13__ originating where it is found

14. meticulous      __17__ perceiving the significance of events before they occur

15. precocious      __2__ a message that departs from the main subject

16. ambiguous      __11__ failing to make or recognize distinctions

17. prescient      __6__ capable of wounding

## Lesson 99           Units 13-15 Review

Can you find all 60 of your vocabulary words in this massive word search? Flip back through the three units for the word list if you need it.

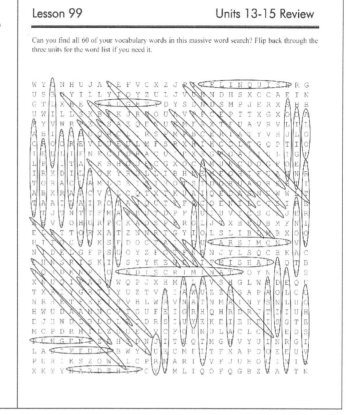

## Lesson 100           Units 13-15 Review Quiz

If you got 100% on all three of your vocabulary quizzes so far, no vocab for you today. Way to go! If you didn't, take this review quiz. If you score higher on this than you did on one of your previous quizzes, you may replace the grade of one of those quizzes on your grade sheet (just one).

Circle the letter that contains the word that *best* fits.

1. We were _____ to the trail of ants coming in overnight.

    a. uninspired    (b.) oblivious    c. haughty    d. obsequious

2. The _____ didn't gel as much as the chemist had anticipated.

    (a.) solution    b. compassion    c. criterion    d. pariah

3. Splitting all the candy was the most _____ thing I could think of.

    a. fastidious    b. fallacious    c. indefatigable    (d.) equitable

4. The toddler didn't want to _____ his sister's toy.

    a. preclude    b. collaborate    (c.) relinquish    d. justify

5. With _____ studying, he received a great score on the SAT.

    a. solipsistic    b. taciturn    (c.) diligent    d. uninspired

Fill in the blank with the word that *best* fits.

6. Showing sustained enthusiastic action is being ___**indefatigable**___.

7. To work together on a common project is to ___**collaborate**___.

8. Characteristic of one eager to fight: ___**belligerent**___.

9. Something intended to deceive is ___**fallacious**___.

10. To restore to a previous or better position is to ___**renovate**___.

## Lesson 101           Units 1-3 Review

Find a partner to help you with this review game. See if you can guess the vocabulary word in ten guesses or less. Guess letters one at a time for each word and have your partner fill them in or let you know they're not in the word.

e x e m p l a r y
Hint: worthy of imitation

d i v e r t
Hint: turn aside

d o c i l e
Hint: easily managed

e x i g e n t
Hint: demanding attention

t r a n s i e n t
Hint: lasting a short time

a c e r b i c
Hint: sour or bitter in taste

d e m e a n o r
Hint: the way a person behaves

d e p i c t
Hint: show in a picture

a b s t r a c t
Hint: existing only in the mind

p r o s a i c
Hint: lacking wit

f r i p p e r y
Hint: something of little value

o r a t o r
Hint: a person who delivers a speech

## Lesson 102           Units 10-12 Review

Match the word to its definition.

| | | |
|---|---|---|
| 1. paragon | 5 | insincerely emotional |
| 2. servile | 7 | concoct something artificial or untrue |
| 3. assimilate | 12 | liveliness and eagerness |
| 4. extol | 3 | become similar to one's environment |
| 5. mawkish | 9 | make obscure or unclear |
| 6. surreptitious | 2 | submissive or fawning in attitude or behavior |
| 7. fabricate | 14 | weaken mentally or morally |
| 8. relegate | 10 | given to lying |
| 9. obfuscate | 16 | extremely steep |
| 10. mendacious | 1 | an ideal instance |
| 11. precarious | 13 | liable to sudden unpredictable change |
| 12. alacrity | 17 | address forcefully |
| 13. mercurial | 4 | praise, glorify, or honor |
| 14. enervate | 8 | assign to a lower position |
| 15. sycophant | 6 | marked by quiet, caution, and secrecy |
| 16. precipitous | 11 | fraught with danger |
| 17. harangue | 15 | a person who tries to please someone for personal gain |

## Lesson 103           Units 4-6 Review

Can you find the listed words from Units 4-6 in this word search? Say the definition as you circle the word. If you can't, go back and look it up before moving on.

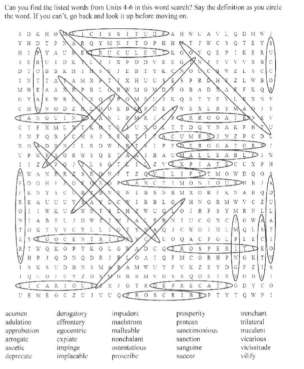

| | | | | |
|---|---|---|---|---|
| acumen | derogatory | impudent | prosperity | trenchant |
| adulation | effrontery | maelstrom | protean | trilateral |
| approbation | egocentric | malleable | sanctimonious | truculent |
| arrogate | expiate | nonchalant | sanction | vicarious |
| ascetic | impinge | ostentatious | sanguine | vicissitude |
| deprecate | implacable | proscribe | succor | vilify |

## Lesson 104           Units 13-15 Review

Fill in the crossword puzzle with words from Units 13-15.

**Across:**
3. failing to keep in mind
8. strong and sharp
11. marked by precise accordance with details
12. originating where it is found
15. a relaxed, comfortable feeling
16. habitually reserved and uncommunicative
17. anything short-lived
19. express strong disapproval of
20. happen to

**Down:**
1. intended to deceive
2. keep from happening or arising
4. never done or known before
5. failing to make distinctions
6. someone who fights
7. believing that only the self exists
9. tendency to believe readily
10. the state of nonexistence
13. lacking powers of invention
14. a small or moderate amount
18. remote in manner

## Lesson 105           Units 7-9 Review

Unscramble your vocabulary words.

**NAXETT**      **extant**
still in existence

**EPLIOCM**      **polemic**
of or involving dispute or controversy

**ISUAUOSSD**      **assiduous**
marked by care and persistent effort

**UCVSSIO**      **viscous**
having a relatively high resistance to flow

**ERMDUBTAA**      **adumbrate**
describe roughly or briefly

**TCCURENIVM**      **circumvent**
beat through cleverness and wit

**URCISOLUSR**      **scurrilous**
expressing offensive reproach

**CDTCASIEE**      **desiccate**
lacking vitality or spirit; lifeless

**SOEISPNAR**      **aspersion**
a disparaging remark

(continued on the next page)

## Lesson 105 — Units 7-9 Review (cont.)

OSOPNAEERUETMX  **extemporaneous**
with little or no preparation or forethought

BUJLTAIN  **jubilant**
joyful and proud especially because of triumph or success

IEALATPL  **palliate**
lessen or try to lessen the seriousness or extent of

LVIUEES  **elusive**
difficult to detect or grasp by the mind

RSITUFE  **surfeit**
supply or feed to fullness

PIDAOSHNUA  **diaphanous**
so thin as to transmit light; see-through

HRPLTAEO  **plethora**
extreme excess

TIUQBUSOUI  **ubiquitous**
being present everywhere at once

LAPDIL  **pallid**
lacking in vitality or interest

PSORUFLEUUS  **superfluous**
serving no useful purpose

NACAAEP  **panacea**
hypothetical remedy for all ills or diseases

## Lesson 109 — Unit 16 Practice

Fill in the crossword puzzle with your vocabulary words. Study for your vocabulary quiz tomorrow. Make sure you know your words. Study ideas: read them out loud, copy the ones you are unsure of, have someone quiz you, use the words in conversation.

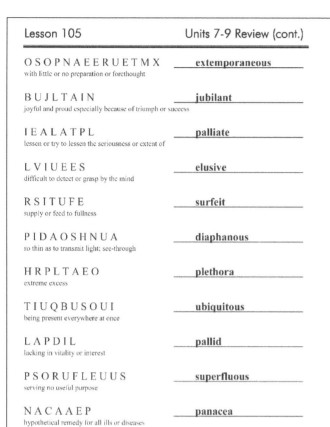

**Across:**
2. no longer in use
5. the state of being held in low esteem
6. an insufficient quantity or number
7. intended to attract notice and impress others
14. express criticism toward
17. teach uncritically
18. take to task
19. make complete or perfect
20. intending to show kindness

**Down:**
1. the dominance of one nation over others
3. liberality in bestowing gifts
4. characterized by friendship
8. kill in large numbers
9. all of something
10. the quality of acting without planning
11. not elegant or graceful in expression
12. producing a sensation of touch
13. a soft, wet area of low-lying land
15. make less severe
16. extremely silly or stupid

## Lesson 110 — Unit 16 Quiz

You can study your words before you take this quiz, but you MUST put them away before you take the quiz. Cheaters get ZERO points for their quiz. Check your answers and record your score on your grade sheet.

Circle the letter that contains the word that *best* fits.

1. Peanut butter and apples _____ each other.
   a. discredit   b. modify   **c. complement**   d. indoctrinate

2. The floppy disk I used to back up my school work is now _____
   a. amicable   b. fatuous   c. cumbersome   **d. obsolete**

3. A _____ learner prefers to be hands-on.
   **a. tactile**   b. pretentious   c. benevolent   d. whole

4. In a moment of complete _____, we drove to the next state just to have lunch.
   a. quagmire   **b. spontaneity**   c. hegemony   d. paucity

5. We used vinegar to try to _____ the pungent odor.
   a. indoctrinate   b. reprove   c. upbraid   **d. eradicate**

Fill in the blank with the word that *best* fits.

6. Being extremely silly or stupid is being ____ **fatuous** ____.

7. The dominance of one nation over others is ____ **hegemony** ____.

8. Creating an appearance of importance is being ____ **pretentious** ____.

9. To express criticism toward is to ____ **upbraid** ____.

10. A synonym for *change* might be ____ **modify** ____.

## Lesson 114 — Unit 17 Practice

Find your vocabulary words in the word search. As you find each one, repeat its definition. Look it up if you can't remember it. Study for your vocabulary quiz tomorrow. Make sure you know your words. Study ideas: read them out loud, copy the ones you are unsure of, have someone quiz you, use the words in conversation.

```
P K J N M Q B Q C Q A D Z K U V J B Y Y E P X P
M B E G Z S D H L P Z O T S F A O R J B K Y N A
F C W H D R G B T V F D W S T G J Y U F N L L
I C E V I T A T I L A U Q N U C E P P P Q
L B A F F E N C Y D Z Y Q I R Z L T M S
G M C U P I D I T Y A N C B N F O H P O L
L H R A N P R L E X C W A U L S S T N
S Z H R Z I S X E T O M E H V E R
R C A K R U J M B N H Q U E A N E B X C L
Z D I B S U I F X E U D R E I A N E Y W D
I L S X G R U O O P O W Z V S P E V U H T
N J G J W B D M N K M O T B C U O T M L
D I L S C E D A O M W M J L Z X H P A L K J U
U E Z C Q T I T S U L W M U J J M M E T K N Z R
X V E U N N D P X M N V G S U T E E X I K
S I E D A W S L M J I F C B W D S G K U B Y X
L T G M X W Z O P A H A A E T D J L Q N Y H
H A O O D C N A P E R C S D N I C S E R A L
L R A E W L M M T L W Q P Q N O G L M Z O D D
X O N E A C U O R E P E R T S B O X X U J S C V
W J R L Y L Z V V N D K F F Z Y J I J D U K H S
T E L O Z A J W U E M Z X F F B L F K R Y W K Z
S P W I H Y U Q E C M O S N I W Q E J A O P E
T G Y L J L T X G U U D B B C U O I R U P S D X
```

anachronism   eschew   momentous   rescind
blandish   fecund   obstreperous   spurious
comply   heinous   pejorative   tantamount
cupidity   ineffable   primeval   usurp
discrepancy   latent   qualitative   winsome

## Lesson 115 — Unit 17 Quiz

You can study your words before you take this quiz, but you MUST put them away before you take the quiz. Cheaters get ZERO points for their quiz. Check your answers and record your score on your grade sheet.

Circle the letter that contains the word that *best* fits.

1. It's hard to _____ with my doctor's orders of no food after 6 p.m.

    a. blandish   **(b.) comply**   c. eschew   d. rescind

2. Another word for cancel is _____.

    a. cupidity   b. anachronism   **(c.) rescind**   d. usurp

3. My dad's request was _____ to a demand.

    a. winsome   b. spurious   c. fecund   **(d.) tantamount**

4. The toddler became _____ after missing her nap.

    a. latent   **(b.) obstreperous**   c. pejorative   d. qualitative

5. A synonym for *avoid*.

    a. blandish   b. rescind   **(c.) eschew**   d. usurp

Fill in the blank with the word that *best* fits.

6. Charming in a childlike way is ___**winsome**___.

7. Plausible but false is ___**spurious**___.

8. Someone who is intellectually productive is ___**fecund**___.

9. Extremely wicked: ___**heinous**___.

10. Defying expression or description: ___**ineffable**___.

## Lesson 119 — Unit 18 Practice

Unscramble your vocabulary words. Study for your vocabulary quiz tomorrow. Make sure you know your words. Study ideas: read them out loud, copy the ones you are unsure of, have someone quiz you, use the words in conversation.

RNSOCTHCIAIAN   ___**anachronistic**___
chronologically misplaced

TPAUOI   ___**utopia**___
ideally perfect state

LIIREPDCPN   ___**principled**___
based on or manifesting objectively defined standards of rightness or morality

IOHRTHTE   ___**hitherto**___
a situation that has existed up to this point or up to the present time

CIDULPEL   ___**pellucid**___
transmitting light; able to be seen through with clarity; easily understandable

ELTRAT   ___**latter**___
the second of two or the second mentioned of two

GENFI   ___**feign**___
make believe with the intent to deceive

RUCYSRO   ___**cursory**___
hasty and without attention to detail

IAETVBENLI   ___**inevitable**___
incapable of being avoided or prevented

(continued on the next page)

## Lesson 119 — Unit 18 Practice (cont.)

SRUTCTBO   ___**obstruct**___
hinder or prevent the progress or accomplishment of

RMOSSA   ___**morass**___
a soft, wet area of low-lying land that sinks underfoot

IATDS   ___**staid**___
characterized by dignity and propriety

STAREEGN   ___**estrange**___
remove from customary environment or associations

TULISFW   ___**wistful**___
showing pensive sadness

EATIUVTTINAQ   ___**quantitative**___
relating to measurement of amount

IENTERLIS   ___**resilient**___
recovering readily from adversity, depression, or the like

ICUERIDSVS   ___**discursive**___
tending to depart from the main point or cover a wide range of subjects

ISTOEUD   ___**tedious**___
so lacking in interest as to cause mental weariness

ROSIMEPCMO   ___**compromise**___
a middle way between two extremes

SEBTRLO   ___**bolster**___
support and strengthen; add padding to

## Lesson 120 — Unit 18 Quiz

You can study your words before you take this quiz, but you MUST put them away before you take the quiz. Cheaters get ZERO points for their quiz. Check your answers and record your score on your grade sheet.

Circle the letter that contains the word that *best* fits.

1. The babbling brook and the shade of the trees made for a sort of _____.

    a. bolster   b. discursive   **(c.) utopia**   d. latter

2. The road closure was _____ once the flooding rains began to fall.

    **(a.) inevitable**   b. pellucid   c. quantitative   d. staid

3. Taking the nails out of the fence was a(n) _____ job.

    a. anachronistic   b. principled   c. wistful   **(d.) tedious**

4. The fence between us helped to _____ my courage as I met my first lion.

    a. compromise   **(b.) bolster**   c. estrange   d. feign

5. A synonym for *mire*.

    a. utopia   **(b.) morass**   c. cursory   d. obstruct

Fill in the blank with the word that *best* fits.

6. Something able to be seen through with clarity is ___**pellucid**___.

7. To hinder or prevent progress is to ___**obstruct**___.

8. Someone who recovers readily from adversity is ___**resilient**___.

9. Characterized by dignity and propriety: ___**staid**___.

10. To make believe with the intent to deceive is to ___**feign**___.

## Lesson 122                      Units 16-18 Review

Find a partner to help you with this review game. See if you can guess the vocabulary word in ten guesses or less. Guess letters one at a time for each word and have your partner fill them in or let you know they're not in the word.

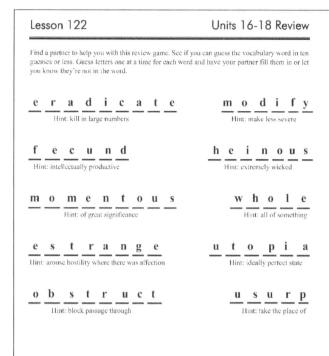

e r a d i c a t e
Hint: kill in large numbers

m o d i f y
Hint: make less severe

f e c u n d
Hint: intellectually productive

h e i n o u s
Hint: extremely wicked

m o m e n t o u s
Hint: of great significance

w h o l e
Hint: all of something

e s t r a n g e
Hint: arouse hostility where there was affection

u t o p i a
Hint: ideally perfect state

o b s t r u c t
Hint: block passage through

u s u r p
Hint: take the place of

## Lesson 123                      Units 16-18 Review

Match the word to its definition.

1. cursory        __2__  extremely silly or stupid
2. fatuous        __8__  express criticism toward
3. anachronism    __5__  tending to depart from the main point
4. obstreperous   __10__ able to be seen through with clarity
5. discursive     __16__ plausible but false
6. morass         __1__  hasty and without attention to detail
7. hegemony       __12__ defying expression or description
8. upbraid        __7__  the dominance of one social group over others
9. cupidity       __13__ liberality in bestowing gifts
10. pellucid      __4__  noisily and stubbornly defiant
11. pejorative    __17__ characterized by dignity and propriety
12. ineffable     __11__ expressing disapproval
13. largess       __3__  something located at a time when it couldn't have existed
14. paucity       __14__ an insufficient quantity or number
15. eschew        __15__ avoid and stay away from deliberately
16. spurious      __6__  a soft, wet area of low-lying land that sinks underfoot
17. staid         __9__  extreme greed for material wealth

## Lesson 124                      Units 16-18 Review

Can you find all 60 of your vocabulary words in this massive word search? Flip back through your three units for the word list if you need it.

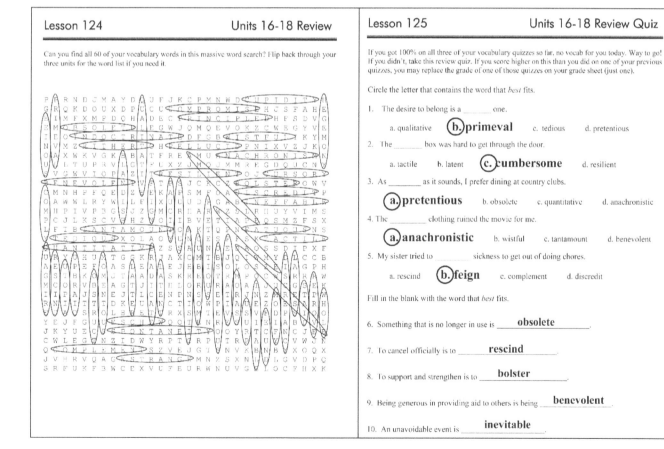

## Lesson 125                      Units 16-18 Review Quiz

If you got 100% on all three of your vocabulary quizzes so far, no vocab for you today. Way to go! If you didn't, take this review quiz. If you score higher on this than you did on one of your previous quizzes, you may replace the grade of one of those quizzes on your grade sheet (just one).

Circle the letter that contains the word that *best* fits.

1. The desire to belong is a _____ one.
   a. qualitative   **b. primeval**   c. tedious   d. pretentious

2. The _____ box was hard to get through the door.
   a. tactile   b. latent   **c. cumbersome**   d. resilient

3. As _____ as it sounds, I prefer dining at country clubs.
   **a. pretentious**   b. obsolete   c. quantitative   d. anachronistic

4. The _____ clothing ruined the movie for me.
   **a. anachronistic**   b. wistful   c. tantamount   d. benevolent

5. My sister tried to _____ sickness to get out of doing chores.
   a. rescind   **b. feign**   c. complement   d. discredit

Fill in the blank with the word that *best* fits.

6. Something that is no longer in use is ____**obsolete**____.

7. To cancel officially is to ____**rescind**____.

8. To support and strengthen is to ____**bolster**____.

9. Being generous in providing aid to others is being ____**benevolent**____.

10. An unavoidable event is ____**inevitable**____.

Fill in the crossword puzzle with your vocabulary words. Study for your vocabulary quiz tomorrow. Make sure you know your words. Study ideas: read them out loud, copy the ones you are unsure of, have someone quiz you, use the words in conversation.

**Across:**
2. break down into components
4. deeply or seriously thoughtful
11. make weak
12. slow to learn or understand
14. having many aspects or qualities
17. wild and menacing
18. stubbornly unyielding
19. complete and confirmed integrity
20. lean and wrinkled by shrinkage as from age or illness

**Down:**
1. having some resemblance
3. tending to vanish like vapor
5. devoid of intelligence or thought
6. an educated guess
7. not in physical motion
8. impervious to reason
9. lacking in rigor or strictness
10. occurring with
13. very close and convivial
15. being in a tense state
16. look down on

---

You can study your words before you take this quiz, but you MUST put them away before you take the quiz. Cheaters get ZERO points for their quiz. Check your answers and record your score on your grade sheet.

Circle the letter that contains the word that *best* fits.

1. I enjoy the _____ sensations of hot apple pie and frigid vanilla ice cream.
   a. feral    b. inexorable    c. vacuous    **d. concomitant**

2. Her face was _____ by age.
   a. quasi    **b. wizened**    c. evanescent    d. boon

3. The _____ people and traditions are what make America great.
   a. evanescent    **b. multifarious**    c. lax    d. quasi

4. The brisk breeze was a _____ to the sweaty sailors.
   **a. boon**    b. hypothesis    c. static    d. probity

5. The _____ recession hit the small business sector hard.
   a. pensive    b. obtuse    **c. tenacious**    d. lax

Fill in the blank with the word that *best* fits.

6. A cat that is not a house pet might be considered ____ **feral** ____.

7. Complete and confirmed integrity is ____ **probity** ____.

8. Something that tends to vanish like vapor is _____ **evanescent** ____.

9. ____ **Static** ____ is a crackling noise caused by electrical interference.

10. An educated guess is a(n) ____ **hypothesis** ____.

---

Find your vocabulary words in the word search. As you find each one, repeat its definition. Look it up if you can't remember it. Study for your vocabulary quiz tomorrow. Make sure you know your words. Study ideas: read them out loud, copy the ones you are unsure of, have someone quiz you, use the words in conversation.

| | | | |
|---|---|---|---|
| anarchy | evince | mundane | restrained |
| brusque | fetid | odious | stolid |
| concurrent | hypothetical | penurious | tenuous |
| decry | informal | proclivity | validate |
| dissemble | legerdemain | quay | zealot |

---

You can study your words before you take this quiz, but you MUST put them away before you take the quiz. Cheaters get ZERO points for their quiz. Check your answers and record your score on your grade sheet.

Circle the letter that contains the word that *best* fits.

1. Many lived a(n) _____ existence after the Great Depression.
   a. concurrent    b. informal    **c. penurious**    d. quay

2. A synonym for *foul* could be _____.
   **a. fetid**    b. brusque    c. stolid    d. tenuous

3. His _____ personality meant he had very few friends.
   a. informal    **b. odious**    c. zealot    d. legerdemain

4. The toddler had a _____ to misbehave.
   a. gargoyle    b. dissemble    c. anarchy    **d. proclivity**

5. I hope my children _____ an attitude of compassion for others.
   **a. evince**    b. decry    c. restrained    d. validate

Fill in the blank with the word that *best* fits.

6. Another word for "slight of hand" is ____ **legerdemain** ____.

7. A wharf usually built parallel to the shoreline is a ____ **quay** ____.

8. Someone who displays very little emotion is ____ **stolid** ____.

9. A state of lawlessness and disorder is known as ____ **anarchy** ____.

10. Things that occur at the same time are ____ **concurrent** ____.

## Lesson 139 — Unit 21 Practice

Unscramble your vocabulary words. Study for your vocabulary quiz tomorrow. Make sure you know your words. Study ideas: read them out loud, copy the ones you are unsure of, have someone quiz you, use the words in conversation.

ETFBFU — **buffet**
strike against forcefully; beat repeatedly

ONISCLAOCT — **iconoclast**
someone who attacks cherished ideas or traditional institutions

FFIOIUOCS — **officious**
intrusive in a meddling or offensive manner

CBRXEEATAE — **exacerbate**
make worse; exasperate or irritate

ENIICNCUMEF — **munificence**
liberality in bestowing gifts; generosity of spirit

UTQIOCXI — **quixotic**
not sensible about practical matters; idealistic and unrealistic

IEFEDL — **defile**
spot, stain, or pollute

HAAMANET — **anathema**
a detested person or thing

REACPTNSARIOT — **procrastinate**
postpone doing what one should be doing

(continued on the next page)

## Lesson 139 — Unit 21 Practice (cont.)

ODRTTEER — **retorted**
answered back

INTEHZ — **zenith**
the highest point

UDRSIFOEIP — **perfidious**
tending to betray

UETSROUSN — **strenuous**
taxing to the utmost

IATMSINEDES — **disseminate**
cause to become widely known

NEDSDGEINCCON — **condescending**
behaving in a patronizing manner

NUEOIUNGS — **ingenuous**
characterized by an inability to mask your feelings

RMTUIOSO — **timorous**
timid by nature or revealing timidity

AVPDI — **vapid**
lacking significance or liveliness of spirit

HRLAIETGC — **lethargic**
deficient in alertness or activity

GETEFLNI — **fleeting**
lasting for a markedly brief time

## Lesson 140 — Unit 21 Quiz

You can study your words before you take this quiz, but you MUST put them away before you take the quiz. Cheaters get ZERO points for their quiz. Check your answers and record your score on your grade sheet.

Circle the letter that contains the word that *best* fits.

1. The waves continued to _____ the side of the boat in the storm.
   **a. buffet**     b. defile     c. procrastinate     d. disseminate

2. After the large meal, we were all feeling a bit _____.
   a. ingenuous     b. fleeting     **c. lethargic**     d. officious

3. Her _____ was widely known among the local charities.
   a. anathema     **b. munificence**     c. iconoclast     d. zenith

4. The _____ entertainment did not keep our attention.
   **a. vapid**     b. timorous     c. strenuous     d. perfidious

5. A synonym for *replied*.
   a. procrastinate     b. exacerbate     **c. retorted**     d. disseminate

Fill in the blank with the word that *best* fits.

6. A detested person or thing is a(n) **anathema**.

7. Tending to betray: **perfidious**.

8. Something that is extremely taxing is **strenuous**.

9. To cause to become widely known is to **disseminate**.

10. Someone who attacks cherished ideas is a(n) **iconoclast**.

## Lesson 142 — Units 19-21 Review

Find a partner to help you with this review game. See if you can guess the vocabulary word in ten guesses or less. Guess letters one at a time for each word and have your partner fill them in or let you know they're not in the word.

p e n u r i o u s
Hint: excessively unwilling to spend

o b t u s e
Hint: slow to learn

e v i n c e
Hint: give expression to

d i s d a i n
Hint: look down on

l e t h a r g i c
Hint: deficient in alertness

f e r a l
Hint: wild

a n a t h e m a
Hint: detested person or thing

d e f i l e
Hint: make dirty

v a l i d a t e
Hint: give evidence for

q u a s i
Hint: having some resemblance

## Lesson 143 — Units 19-21 Review

Match the word to its definition.

| | | |
|---|---|---|
| 1. buffet | 3 | a natural inclination |
| 2. quixotic | 10 | tending to betray |
| 3. proclivity | 8 | complete and confirmed integrity |
| 4. tenuous | 17 | timid by nature |
| 5. debilitate | 2 | idealistic and unrealistic |
| 6. inexorable | 11 | lacking in taste or flavor |
| 7. evanescent | 7 | tending to vanish like vapor |
| 8. probity | 14 | marked by rude or peremptory shortness |
| 9. stolid | 1 | beat repeatedly |
| 10. perfidious | 13 | deeply or seriously thoughtful |
| 11. vapid | 15 | an illusory feat |
| 12. dissemble | 4 | lacking substance or significance |
| 13. pensive | 9 | not easily aroused or excited |
| 14. brusque | 16 | liberality in bestowing gifts |
| 15. legerdemain | 5 | make weak |
| 16. munificence | 12 | hide under a false appearance |
| 17. timorous | 6 | impervious to pleas or reason |

## Lesson 144 — Units 19-21 Review

Can you find all 60 of your vocabulary words in this massive word search? Flip back through your three units for the word list if you need it.

## Lesson 145 — Units 19-21 Review Quiz

If you got 100% on all three of your vocabulary quizzes so far, no vocab for you today. Way to go! If you didn't, take this review quiz. If you score higher on this than you did on one of your previous quizzes, you may replace the grade of one of those quizzes on your grade sheet (just one).

Circle the letter that contains the word that *best* fits.

1. A synonym for *smelly*.

a. multifarious   b. vacuous   c. officious   **(d.) fetid**

2. The baby held my finger in his _____ little fist.

**(a.) tenacious**   b. odious   c. ingenuous   d. strenuous

3. If you _____ too much you'll miss out on our weekend plans.

a. exacerbate   **(b.) procrastinate**   c. disseminate   d. decry

4. The _____ task of raking the leaves was somehow soothing to me.

**(a.) mundane**   b. hypothetical   c. concurrent   d. wizened

5. Their _____ expressions told me it was time to end the lecture.

a. multifarious   b. officious   **(c.) vacuous**   d. strenuous

Fill in the blank with the word that *best* fits.

6. A state of lawlessness and disorder: **anarchy**

7. Having many aspects or qualities is known as **multifarious**

8. Something that's unequivocally detestable is **odious**

9. To cause to become widely known is to **disseminate**

10. The highest point is the **zenith**

## Lesson 149 — Unit 22 Practice

Fill in the crossword puzzle with your vocabulary words. Study for your vocabulary quiz tomorrow. Make sure you know your words. Study ideas: read them out loud, copy the ones you are unsure of, have someone quiz you, use the words in conversation.

**Across:**
1. not thorough
6. short account of an incident
11. slow and apathetic
13. lacking foresight or scope
15. grow and flourish
18. existing as an essential characteristic
19. something subject to change
20. disagreeing, especially with a majority

**Down:**
2. feeling of great annoyance
3. a feeling of deep and bitter anger
4. elaborately or excessively ornamented
5. harmful to living things
7. consider hallowed or exalted
8. a slight wind, usually refreshing
9. demanding strict attention to rules
10. a state at a particular time
12. showing knowledge and skill
14. lacking moral discipline
16. leave undone or leave out
17. contrary to accepted morality

## Lesson 150 — Unit 22 Quiz

You can study your words before you take this quiz, but you MUST put them away before you take the quiz. Cheaters get ZERO points for their quiz. Check your answers and record your score on your grade sheet.

Circle the letter that contains the word that *best* fits.

1. Having a low level of vitamin D can be _____ to your health.
   **a. deleterious**   b. florid   c. illicit   d. proficient

2. In late spring, the weeds in our yard _____ and take over if we don't tend to them.
   a. omit   b. condition   **c. burgeon**   d. reverence

3. A synonym for immoral could be _____.
   a. florid   b. inherent   c. perfunctory   **d. licentious**

4. In my _____ I let out a huge sigh.
   a. zephyr   **b. exasperation**   c. anecdote   d. variable

5. California is a state with _____ air pollution guidelines.
   a. torpid   **b. stringent**   c. perfunctory   d. myopic

Fill in the blank with the word that *best* fits.

6. A feeling of deep and bitter anger and ill-will is ___**rancor**___

7. A short account of an incident is known as a(n) ___**anecdote**___

8. Something slow and apathetic is ___**torpid**___

9. Something marked by diversity or difference ___**variable**___

10. Elaborately or excessively ornamented is known as ___**florid**___

---

## Lesson 154 — Unit 23 Practice

Find your vocabulary words in the word search. As you find each one, repeat its definition. Look it up if you can't remember it. Study for your vocabulary quiz tomorrow. Make sure you know your words. Study ideas: read them out loud, copy the ones you are unsure of, have someone quiz you, use the words in conversation.

```
K Q R Z E T W I J C C M Y R I A D F G T I Y
O I T F R K A S V F Z P X N J N U O R D I P
R Q C D F D K Y P P H S O Q I B G R D K J P
Q W V Q F K B H S U V A E D H G G T T R G M
J J O K W X O Z E S D V N D J S E U O W N D
K A N Y R W H R U I S Y J W W I H U E J
T X E R Y R C W Z B E P A Z M I L O T A X E Y
Z C T A M Y W Z B E P A Z M I L O T U P D
V A G C O E U N K Q J P M X D T U X S E L
S F A M R U T T E P R O L I F I C S W Q U
I M N M M F L A U B N I Y I S T U P E F Y
I F L W E A P B E A E S E O P Q Y T T R M
H D Y M G O N C A L I Y R N G C G I Z X S N
F F N Z G G R S M T A V I G V J O B I J C I
Z Y D F K W Y O E N Q L P K G H A A S C O P
Q O U J W E V Z Z R N X A W L R I A N C O
F C I R I I K O X L I M P I D N J S L J T
A R I E G A T E J G E W S Z R M I K Z J E
R N P B G E E R E G O D D G B U Z H N Z N R N
K D E A F L R U M M F Z P P U E S L L X C
F E M L I N R I L R W N L B K M A C T E Z I C
K K I U A Q K G W G I N I M I C A D E S F
Y U U O N M X E J T O O N G I T C M X L D I T
```

| | | | |
|---|---|---|---|
| anonymous | exculpate | myriad | ribald |
| burnish | fortuitous | omnipotent | stupefy |
| conditional | immense | perpetual | tractable |
| demagogue | inimical | prolific | variegated |
| dither | limpid | rancorous | zest |

---

## Lesson 155 — Unit 23 Quiz

You can study your words before you take this quiz, but you MUST put them away before you take the quiz. Cheaters get ZERO points for their quiz. Check your answers and record your score on your grade sheet.

Circle the letter that contains the word that *best* fits.

1. The _____ tip helped the police find the missing car.
   a. conditional   b. inimical   **c. anonymous**   d. prolific

2. A series of _____ circumstances helped advance his political career.
   **a. fortuitous**   b. rancorous   c. omnipotent   d. limpid

3. A terrible and _____ argument erupted.
   a. conditional   b. variegated   c. tractable   **d. rancorous**

4. Alyssa rushed out of the room in an apparent _____.
   a. demagogue   **b. dither**   c. burnish   d. zest

5. The headlights seemed to _____ the deer.
   **a. stupefy**   b. exculpate   c. zest   d. dither

Fill in the blank with the word that *best* fits.

6. To polish and make shiny is to ___**burnish**___

7. To pronounce not guilty of criminal charges is to ___**exculpate**___

8. Something that is clear and bright is ___**limpid**___

9. Continuing forever or indefinitely is known as ___**perpetual**___

10. To make senseless or dizzy is to ___**stupefy**___

---

## Lesson 159 — Unit 24 Practice

Unscramble your vocabulary words. Study for your vocabulary quiz tomorrow. Make sure you know your words. Study ideas: read them out loud, copy the ones you are unsure of, have someone quiz you, use the words in conversation.

S U E R — ___**ruse**___
a deceptive maneuver, especially to avoid capture

R A I D N — ___**nadir**___
an extreme state of adversity

I A T R T — ___**trait**___
a distinguishing feature

O T Y O Z — ___**zooty**___
flashy in manner or style

M N A E D E — ___**demean**___
reduce in worth or character, usually verbally

L E P X E P R — ___**perplex**___
be a mystery or bewildering to

T B R S S U T E — ___**buttress**___
to make stronger or defensible

I I E N T M M N — ___**imminent**___
close in time; about to occur

Y U Q I I T N I — ___**iniquity**___
morally objectionable behavior

(continued on the next page)

## Lesson 159 — Unit 24 Practice (cont.)

BOBLYSTI — **lobbyist**
someone employed to persuade legislators to vote in a way that favors their employer

BMUERSEG — **submerge**
sink below the surface

IVNETRGDE — **divergent**
moving apart from a standard

ECREAEXLB — **execrable**
of very poor quality or condition

URSIFOCTA — **fractious**
stubbornly resistant to authority or control

NREPOOUPT — **opportune**
suitable or at a time that is advantageous

RCIAELSIT — **realistic**
aware or expressing awareness of things as they really are

NLERVEEAB — **venerable**
impressive by reason of age

OTTINASANG — **antagonist**
someone who offers opposition

LEDCNCNEOO — **condolence**
an expression of sympathy with another's grief

MGLPUAOTRE — **promulgate**
state or announce

## Lesson 160 — Unit 24 Quiz

You can study your words before you take this quiz, but you MUST put them away before you take the quiz. Cheaters get ZERO points for their quiz. Check your answers and record your score on your grade sheet.

Circle the letter that contains the word that *best* fits.

1. The novel's _____ was the protagonist's brother.
   a. buttress    b. lobbyist    **c. antagonist**    d. nadir

2. The coach was known to _____ his players when they were losing a game.
   **a. demean**    b. submerge    c. perplex    d. promulgate

3. The celebrity's _____ outfit drew the media's attention.
   a. realistic    b. imminent    **c. zooty**    d. divergent

4. She can tell a storm is _____ due to the aches in her bones.
   a. execrable    b. fractious    c. venerable    **d. imminent**

5. A synonym for *bewilder*.
   a. promulgate    b. submerge    c. buttress    **d. perplex**

Fill in the blank with the word that *best* fits.

6. An expression of sympathy with another's grief: **condolence**.

7. Someone who is stubbornly resistant to authority is **fractious**.

8. An extreme state of adversity is **nadir**.

9. A distinguishing feature is known as a(n) **trait**.

10. To state or announce is to **promulgate**

## Lesson 162 — Units 22-24 Review

Find a partner to help you with this review game. See if you can guess the vocabulary word in ten guesses or less. Guess letters one at a time for each word and have your partner fill them in or let you know they're not in the word.

r e v e r e n c e
Hint: consider hallowed

m y r i a d
Hint: countless

l i m p i d
Hint: clear and bright

b u r n i s h
Hint: polish

e x c u l p a t e
Hint: pronounce not guilty

n a d i r
Hint: lowest point

a n e c d o t e
Hint: short account of an incident

m y o p i c
Hint: lacking foresight

i n i q u i t y
Hint: unjust act

t r a i t
Hint: distinguishing feature

## Lesson 163 — Units 22-24 Review

Match the word to its definition.

1. deleterious — __6__ a deceptive maneuver
2. licentious — __11__ moving apart from a standard
3. inimical — __2__ lacking moral discipline
4. prolific — __13__ grow and flourish
5. imminent — __1__ harmful to living things
6. ruse — __8__ slow and apathetic
7. tractable — __12__ make senseless or dizzy
8. torpid — __5__ about to occur
9. illicit — __14__ great in size
10. dither — __17__ continuing indefinitely
11. divergent — __7__ easily managed
12. stupefy — __15__ make more complicated
13. burgeon — __4__ intellectually productive
14. immense — __16__ flashy in manner or style
15. perplex — __10__ act nervously
16. zooty — __3__ not friendly
17. perpetual — __9__ forbidden by law

## Lesson 164        Units 22-24 Review

Can you find all 60 of your vocabulary words in this massive word search? Flip back through your three units for the word list if you need it.

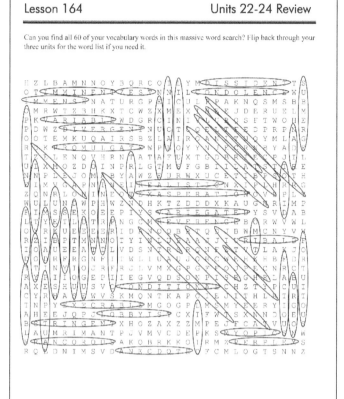

## Lesson 165        Units 22-24 Review Quiz

If you got 100% on all three of your vocabulary quizzes so far, no vocab for you today. Way to go! If you didn't, take this review quiz. If you score higher on this than you did on one of your previous quizzes, you may replace the grade of one of those quizzes on your grade sheet (just one).

Circle the letter that contains the word that *best* fits.

1. The _____ snowstorms kept us home for weeks.
      a. perfunctory    **b. perpetual**    c. ribald    d. opportune

2. My _____ rug adds life to the room.
      a. rancorous    b. perfunctory    **c. variegated**    d. stringent

3. The athlete lifted weights to _____ his body.
      **a. condition**    b. omit    c. demean    d. promulgate

4. You need to _____ the chicken in the broth to keep it from drying out.
      **a. submerge**    b. ribald    c. demagogue    d. zephyr

5. His teenager answered most questions with _____ nods.
      a. omnipotent    b. anonymous    **c. perfunctory**    d. florid

Fill in the blank with the word that *best* fits.

6. Vigorous and enthusiastic enjoyment is _____ **zest** _____.

7. Something of very poor quality is _____ **execrable** _____.

8. Stubbornly resistant to authority or control is _____ **fractious** _____.

9. A synonym for *exclude* might be _____ **omit** _____.

10. A feeling of great annoyance is known as _____ **exasperation** _____.

## Lesson 166        Units 16-18 Review

Find a partner to help you with this review game. See if you can guess the vocabulary word in ten guesses or less. Guess letters one at a time for each word and have your partner fill them in or let you know they're not in the word.

m o m e n t o u s
Hint: of great significance

m o r a s s
Hint: mire

l a t t e r
Hint: the second of two

h e i n o u s
Hint: extremely wicked

d i s c r e d i t
Hint: damage the reputation of dignity

s t a i d
Hint: characterized by

p r i m e v a l
Hint: in an earliest state

c o m p l y
Hint: act in accordance with rules

f a t u o u s
Hint: extremely silly

r e p r o v e
Hint: admonish

a m i c a b l e
Hint: friendly

u t o p i a
Hint: ideally perfect state

## Lesson 167        Units 10-12 Review

Match the word to its definition.

1. coalesce    _8_   concoct something artificial or untrue
2. hapless    _3_   liveliness and eagerness
3. alacrity    _13_   praise, glorify, or honor
4. solicitous    _6_   insincerely emotional
5. puerile    _17_   a difficult problem
6. mawkish    _5_   displaying a lack of maturity
7. assimilate    _12_   a perfect embodiment of a concept
8. fabricate    _15_   weaken mentally or morally
9. cogent    _1_   fuse together
10. vituperate    _16_   make unclear
11. vitriolic    _10_   spread negative information about
12. paragon    _7_   become similar to one's environment
13. extol    _4_   full of anxiety and concern
14. mendacious    _14_   given to lying
15. enervate    _9_   powerfully persuasive
16. obfuscate    _11_   harsh or corrosive in tone
17. conundrum    _2_   inciting pity

## Lesson 168      Units 1-3 Review

Can you find the listed words from Units 1-3 in this word search? Say the definition as you circle the word. If you can't, go back and look it up before moving on.

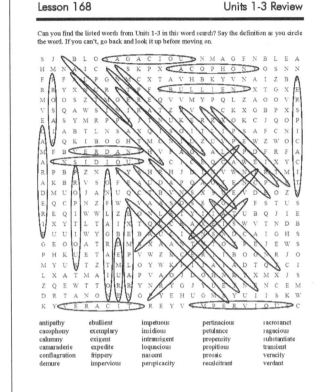

| antipathy | ebullient | impetuous | pertinacious | sacrosanct |
| cacophony | exemplary | insidious | petulance | sagacious |
| calumny | exigent | intransigent | propensity | substantiate |
| camaraderie | expedite | loquacious | propitious | transient |
| conflagration | frippery | nascent | prosaic | veracity |
| demure | impervious | perspicacity | recalcitrant | verdant |

## Lesson 169      Units 13-15 Review

Fill in the crossword puzzle with words from Units 13-15.

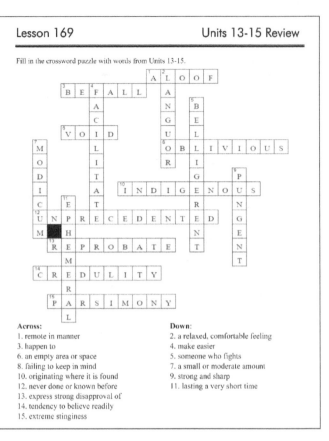

**Across:**
1. remote in manner
3. happen to
6. an empty area or space
8. failing to keep in mind
10. originating where it is found
12. never done or known before
13. express strong disapproval of
14. tendency to believe readily
15. extreme stinginess

**Down:**
2. a relaxed, comfortable feeling
4. make easier
5. someone who fights
7. a small or moderate amount
9. strong and sharp
11. lasting a very short time

## Lesson 170      Units 4-6 Review

Unscramble your vocabulary words.

**CAENMU**      _acumen_
shrewdness shown by keen insight

**IALTDNUOA**      _adulation_
exaggerated and hypocritical praise

**EARTPEDEC**      _deprecate_
belittle; express strong disapproval of

**PIEXTEA**      _expiate_
make amends for

**EENPYOHT**      _neophyte_
a new participant in some activity; someone young or inexperienced

**ANTCEHNTR**      _trenchant_
clearly or sharply defined to the mind

**ATGOARRE**      _arrogate_
assert one's right to

**LPCAEIMLAB**      _implacable_
incapable of being appeased

**LCNANHONTA**      _nonchalant_
marked by blithe unconcern

(continued on the next page)

## Lesson 170      Units 4-6 Review

**SSNOEBTIEL**      _ostensible_
appearing as such but not necessarily so; pretended

**TYPIH**      _pithy_
concise and full of meaning

**CCOSUR**      _succor_
help in a difficult situation

**RESTDCAEE**      _desecrate_
violate the sacred character of a place or language

**NEGUXPE**      _expunge_
remove by erasing or crossing out or as if by drawing a line

**LPTUTDAEI**      _platitude_
a trite or obvious remark

**TTCUNELUR**      _truculent_
defiantly aggressive

**ERCIOBRPS**      _proscribe_
command against

**RTYROEDAGO**      _derogatory_
expressive of low opinion

**IEURN**      _inure_
cause to accept or become hardened to; habituate

**ENIGSNUA**      _sanguine_
confidently optimistic and cheerful